FOOD IN CIVILIZATION
How History Has Been Affected
By Human Tastes

Also by the author

ART OF THE ESKIMO

THE DECORATED GUN

FRONTIER PARISH:
An Account of the Society for the Propagation
of the Gospel & the Anglican Church in
America, Drawn from the Records of the
Bishop of London

MAKING SCIENTIFIC TOYS

ROCK ART OF AFRICA

SOFT STONE CARVING

ART IN PAPER

FOOD IN CIVILIZATION

How History Has Been Affected
By Human Tastes

CARSON I. A. RITCHIE

BEAUFORT BOOKS, INC.
New York/Toronto

Library of Congress Cataloging in Publication Data
Ritchie, Carson I. A.
  Food in civilization
  1. Food — History.   2. Civilization — History.
I.   Title.
TX353.R54   1981   338.1′9   81-4288
ISBN 0-8253-0037-1   AACR2

Printed in the United States by Beaufort Books, Inc., New York.
Published simultaneously in Canada by Nelson, Foster and Scott Ltd.
Printed in the U.S.A.   First Edition
10 9 8 7 6 5 4 3 2 1

CONTENTS

INTRODUCTION

I once took some friends out for a meal at a grand café. We all ordered — rather lavishly — and enjoyed ourselves hugely. Everything went well until the bill arrived, when I put my hand in my pocket and found — not enough money.

Fortunately my friends had money, and I was able to borrow from them to cover my obligations. But later I thought that the history of food is a little like my experience: When it comes time to pay for the feast, we may find that it cost us more than we were prepared to pay.

I did not set out to write this book to demonstrate that the quest for food had tended to bring down untold misfortunes on mankind. But this is what did happen in many cases. Almost the first thing *Homo sapiens* did when he appeared on the stage of history was to exterminate his predecessor the Neanderthal in a disagreement about the allocation of dwindling food supplies. The search for spices helped to bring about the collapse of the Roman Empire and with it Western civilization. When that civilization was reborn at the Renaissance, it was to begin the process of colonization and enslavement all over again — still on the hunt for spices.

The sugar to sweeten European tea and coffee was grown only at the cost of black slavery. Indians were ruthlessly pushed off their prairie hunting grounds so that white men could grow wheat and corn, their buffalo slaughtered to make room for cattle. American writers have accused the big fruit companies of wreaking havoc with Central American economies, constructing railroads illegally, omitting to pay taxes, driving down the price of labor (low enough to begin with), expropriating peasant proprietors, and using up the fertility of the soil — just to put bananas on American tables.

Yet, though it is possible to regard the story of food in history as one disastrous course after another, we ought to remember that, while some of the guests have behaved very badly, the long banquet has given others an opportunity of behaving equally well. It is not what you eat but how you eat it. Or as the philosopher Epictetus remarked, even an ordinary event like a dinner can be carried out in such a way as to show friendship and brotherhood with other men.

Many of those bidden to the human feast have behaved in this spirit, men like Sir Philip Sidney, who was offered a cup of water while he lay dying after the battle of Zutphen, but who handed the cup to a wounded soldier lying beside him, and said, "Friend, your need is greater than mine." We can sympathize with those who saw hunger as an opportunity for doing practical good, such as the American-born Sir Benjamin Thompson, Count Rumford, who spent his life looking for ways of enabling the poor to cook their food more economically and invented packet food as a sort of by-product of the process. We can certainly find inspiration in the lives of great pioneers like Captain Cook, who tried to eliminate the dreadful disease scurvy by giving his seamen lemon juice and sauerkraut and added a new continent to the map, Australasia, in the process.

So this is a book about food, its good effects and bad, from ancient times through the twentieth century. It is hoped that the reader will find fresh insights into his own history and his attitudes toward what he eats.

Above all, readers ought to come away from this book with the feeling that food is *important,* that it is not something that happens, off stage, away from the main action, in what is called social history. In the old days when watches were not driven by a battery, you could open the back of a watch and see a multitude of little wheels. Yet there was one wheel, bigger than the rest, the flywheel, which was in turn driven by the most important component of the watch, the mainspring. Food is very much the mainspring of the human watch. Nobody can live long without eating. Along with the ordinary bodily functions, it is the only universal attribute of all human beings. There seems some evidence that food is becoming much more important in our lives. Take the amount of time it consumes. It seems safe to assume that the meals of *Homo sapiens* never lasted as long as, say, a White House banquet. In England the staple of conversation used to be the weather; nowadays it is the price of food.

Just because eating is a universal human attribute, I make no apology for omitting much. It is impossible to give an account of the food habits of the whole of mankind, and if it were, it would be extremely tedious to do it.

In this book I have tried very hard to concentrate on the mainstream history of food. Though many aspects of food are attractive, I have ruthlessly avoided them. I have left out the artistic aspects of food — I have said almost nothing about dietetics, which is so important that all people ought to study it for themselves.

Mainly I have concentrated on the effect that food has had on history. It is the *misconceptions* about food, not the correct assumptions, that have had the greatest importance. Beliefs that spices enhance virility, that sugar is essential to health, and that to be strong you must drink beer have done much more to shape the destinies of mankind than the genuine, demonstrable laws of the science of eating.

It is in this very irrationality, I feel, that the fascination of food's effect on history lies. Man is an aberrant animal who has abandoned his natural feeding habits. Much of his food history is quite unaccountable to reason. Many of the menus of the past are baffling to modern tastes. In the end we must face up to the conclusion that eating is a psychological, not a physiological necessity. Therefore we must suspend our judgment of mankind and its follies of the past as we follow it in its pursuit of food through the ages.

1.

The Hunting Revolution

MAN'S EARLIEST DIET

Food first started to exercise a decisive influence on human history some two million years ago when a subman called *Australopithecus* or "Southern Ape," underwent a permanent change in posture from all fours to erectness. The diet of the hominids that preceded *Australopithecus* had been sparse and uninteresting. These hominids had been food gatherers, not hunters, and what they found to hand in the all-fours position was berries, fruits and nuts, young shoots, roots and bulbs, insects and larvae, worms, the eggs of ground-nesting birds, reptiles, and small mammals.

This was an uninteresting bill of fare compared with what could be obtained by a little effort, such as a stretching up into the upright position. Some anthropologists will have it that the new change of posture had nothing to do with food, but was an attempt to obtain a better all-around view from a higher position, or to wield a stick. Hitherto the hominids' most prominent natural weapons had been his projecting canine teeth. These had ceased to push out as aggressively as once they had over the last few hundred thousand years. With their passing, man now felt more defenseless, and this was why he felt obliged to stand erect and wield a club.

What ought not to be forgotten is that the canine teeth might have been equally useful as an eating tool. I am therefore convinced that the great change was inspired to some extent by appetite. Man probably felt compelled to get up on his hind legs, *so as to have the use of two hands* to carry out some eating process. An erect stance would enable him to pry out of its shell one of those large land snails which are still a feature of South Africa, where he was very much at home. Uprightness would also bring within reach fruits on thin overhanging boughs or enable him to swoop down on some swiftly moving reptile or mammal. In fact, a whole host of dietary habits can best be carried out in an upright position, such as, for example, stripping all the bark off a tree, to secure the grubs beneath it, or snatching delicious honeycombs from a hive with the left hand while beating off hordes of indignant bees with the right.

Whether it is merely a case of *post hoc sed non propter hoc* (after, not because) is difficult to say, but there can be no doubt that erectness widely extended *Australopithecus'* menu. Instead of being merely a food-gatherer, he now became a hunter. Armed with the advantage of gravity acquired by a higher stance, upright man could kill his prey, mainly antelopes, horses, and giraffes, by braining them with large stones which he hurled. He could also deliver telling blows with the shoulder blades of the animals he had eaten, and stab with deadly effect with their sharp horns.

The change from the largely vegetarian diet of the early hominids to a largely meat diet had profound effects on upright man. Everything about his environment and habits changed. It was as if the reach for an upright stance had been a biological allegory of the eating of the Forbidden Fruit in Eden. Man came out from the trees, which had been his original habitat, into the open, looking for game. A hunter must have a base, to which he can return with his catch and where he will rendezvous with his fellow hunters. So man acquired his first home — the top of a rounded granite hill, of the kind called *kopjes* in Africa, or perhaps a rock shelter, a shallow recess in the face of a cliff from which he could keep a constant lookout for the movement of game.

His eyes sharpened in pursuit of the quarry; he began to run faster in its pursuit and also to think more quickly. The cooperative efforts of a team were required to drive the fast running antelopes into some area where they could be ambushed or otherwise brought down, such as the edge of a precipice. Then when an antelope herd had fallen to its death, it was necessary to organize a retrival party to climb down, skin the animal, cut up the meat, and bring it back to base. Processes such as these hastened, if they did not create, the birth of language. It was necessary for someone to give orders, thus promoting a stronger organization in the human group. The question of who was to receive which particular part of the kill had to be worked out as a decision, and then developed into a custom with all the sacrosanct authority of immemorial practice. Even nowadays in primitive hunting societies there is a part of the carcass for every individual. Nobody is left out, but the order of choice is rigidly laid down, with the choice morsels going to the head of the group. There are never any arguments about sharing, because each knows his place.

THE ECOLOGICAL REVOLUTION

All these changes, coming together in such a short time, had effected in man what is known as an ecological revolution. Animals hunt by instinct, but their instinct programs them to hunt for a particular kind of prey. By abandoning his original food gathering for a hunting diet, man had left instinct behind him, and he now had to work out everything for himself. So he began to acquire a sharper intelligence and a larger brain to cope with the new problems forced on him by a change of diet.

Life now became a great process of trial and error. Just how man escaped extinction during his experiments with additions to his diet we shall never know. The larder of nature swarms with poisonous delicacies — such as the liver of the arctic bear, for example — that man had to learn to avoid. Presumably *Australopithecus* taught himself to watch carefully what other creatures devoured with impunity. This is not an absolutely safe rule (a hawk can devour enough strychnine to kill a regiment and show no ill effects), but it was a good working guide. The labors of hyenas to chew through the bones of large animals may then have directed upright man to what was to prove his real dietary treat — marrow. So a new science was born, animal behavior.

The change to a meat diet undoubtedly made man more productive, and probably altered his whole physique for the better. In support of this claim dieticians would point to the extraordinary changes in height that set in in Japan at the beginning of the Meiji Era (1867 – 1912). Confined by Buddhist beliefs to a diet of cereals, vegetables, and fish (fish do not have blood, say Buddhists, and are therefore not living creatures) the Japanese had had an average height of four foot five inches. With the introduction of meat into the diet their height increased considerably.

Countries with purely vegetarian diets, such as India, are notorious for low productivity.

But there are drawbacks to a meat diet, as every vegetarian will explain. In the case of early man one of these drawbacks took the form of a dependency on salt. This dependency was acquired by eating the salt present in meat. If he ever abandoned a meat diet, or cut down the amount of meat he normally ate, man would have to seek out extra supplies of salt, to compensate. Ever since the days of *Australopithecus* man has become addicted to salt; he cannot live without it.

CANNABALISM

A more serious consequence of the change to a meat diet was the appearance, for the first time, of cannibalism. Amongst the broken bones and skulls found in association with *Australopithecus'* remains were several skulls which had been deliverately broken into by a blow administered from the front, or aimed at the left temple. Had this operation been carried out to obtain the brain, a choice morsel? The most we can do is to return a verdict of "not proven" against *Australopithecus*. He may have wanted to remove the cranial content of the skull for some very good reason. Many primitive people, such as the Australian aborigines, carry the bones and skulls of their dead relatives around with them. It is much easier to do this if the skull has been picked clean by scraping it out, or exposing it to voracious insects, such as ants.

Whether or not it did begin at this stage of human development or not, cannibalism crops up from time to time throughout history, under many different forms. Sometimes the cannibal is an aberrant criminal, like Sawnery Bean, a sixteenth-century marauder who waylaid travellers in Angus, in Scotland, killed them, and devoured them in his cave. Long after he had met his just desserts, his daughter too reverted to cannibalism, and was burned alive in Dundee, saying to the crowd as she died: "If ye should taste men's flesh ye would think nothing sweeter." Whole groups of people became cannibals because they longed for the protein in meat but could not obtain it. The Maoris of New Zealand were never able to acquire meat until the pig was introduced into Polynesia and Australasia by Captain Cook (1728 – 79). Because they were protein-starved, they indulged in cannibalism, but they only ate their enemies.

Cannibalism, too, can be ceremonial — a magical act designed to communicate to the eater the qualities and powers of him who furnished the feast. Captain James Cook fell a victim to this kind of cannibalism. After he had been killed by the Hawaiians in a skirmish he was devoured by his enemies who wished to acquire the *mana* or magical power that they attributed to the great navigator. No greater gesture of respect could have been paid in Polynesia. Likewise, when Father Jean de Brébeuf and his companions were martyred during the Huron war (Ontario, 1649), the Iroquois so admired their victims for enduring hours of atrocious torture that they cut out and ate their hearts — believed to be the source of human courage.

Whatever form it took, cannibalism was a direct consequence of the change to a meat diet. Apes do not eat one another, apparently because they have never acquired the taste for meat.

BIRTH OF COOKING: PEKING MAN

Another direct consequence of the change to meat was the birth of cooking, for which *Australopithecus'* successor, Peking Man, was apparently responsible. This ancient inhabitant of China was a broad-nosed, high-cheekboned stocky fellow about five feet tall (five inches taller, be it noted, than the pre-Meiji Japanese). Beneath his craggy, apelike eyebrows darted bright, intelligent eyes, for he had a much better developed brain than had his predecessor. The floor of his cave home was littered with the bones of really formidable adversaries he had overcome: the tiger, the buffalo, the rhinoceros, the prehistoric elephant, the wild horse, the gazelle, and the ostrich.

The wood fire which was Peking Man's *batterie de cuisine* had apparently been invented as a consequence of his manufacture of flint tools. A flint hand ax or knife, carelessly struck in the wrong place by a hammer stone, emitted a spark which had fallen on the bed on which the ax-maker slept, a bed of dry leaves, and set it on fire. The invention of fire came all the more timely in that the climate was becoming much colder. As the world moved slowly toward an Ice Age, the animals on which Peking Man lived had acquired a coat of long hair. Their flesh, left out in the snow, would have become so frozen as to be uneatable. Yet the fire stood ready at hand. Built for warmth against the cold, it became an apparatus first for thawing, then for cooking food.

Vegetarians have little need to cook their food, though most of them do. Most vegetables can be grated and eaten raw. But there is a psychological feeling of well-being engendered in us by hot food — a recollection, perhaps, of mother's milk.

Though even nowadays the Japanese eat raw fish and the Germans raw meat, cooking is a necessity for most meat eaters. It kills bacteria, which may be present in the meat, and it arrests the processes of decay which would otherwise make the flesh uneatable in a very short time. Cooked meat can be kept for a day or two, except in very warm climates. Cooking also improves the appearance of meat, and most important perhaps from the point of view of Peking Man, it breaks up the tissues and removes some of the toughness from the original joint. There is no comparision between the tenderness of a cut from a domesticated animal and that of a wild one. Explorer John Hanning Speke (1827 – 64) said that to imagine the meals he ate from the game animals he shot during his travels in Africa, the reader had to ''think of the toughest steak you have ever eaten, multiply by ten, and subtract the gravy.'' Nowadays it is usual to ''hang'' game. Pheasants, hares, and venison are laid aside in a larder to let the processes of decomposition begin and soften the meat. This process was unsuitable for Peking Man, partly because of the cold climate, but more because there were too many rivals for his food supplies, such as bears which might be attracted by the scent of the decomposing meat and invade his cave.

Peking Man's efforts at cookery were very rudimentary. They seem to have been confined to straightforward roasting, with the joints of meat laid right on the embers. Some have even doubted his ability to cook at all, on the grounds that bones are still broken to get out the marrow, whereas you can (supposedly) simply liquefy the marrow over the fire and pour it out. I know no marrow melters myself. Anyone I know who eats marrow saws or breaks the bone and then scoops out the marrow with a spoon.

NEANDERTHAL MAN AND HIS DIET

Any shortcomings in cooking that were observable in Peking Man were made up by his successor. Neanderthal Man appeared during two spells of extreme cold in the Age of Glaciers, some 75,000 years before our era. He was very widely distributed, not just in Germany from where he gets his name, but in many other parts of Europe and even Asia. Although the Neanderthalers are described by anthropologists as having sloping foreheads, pugnacious jaws, forbidding eyebrow ridges, and gangling gaits, their appearance may not have been so very different from our own. One of the bodies excavated from the Norse settlement at Brattahlid in Greenland has been hailed as that of a man identical with the Neanderthalers, though there has been some controversy on this subject.

There seems every reason to think that the Neanderthalers may have known their hard times. Some of them apparently suffered from rickets — a disease caused by a shortage of Vitamin D. A disease such as this could be brought on by lack of sunlight, and during the Ice Age there were long periods of rainy weather in unglaciated areas, or it might have been induced by an insufficiency of animal food containing the natural sterols which would be an antidote to the disease.

Probably food was scarce, because it is difficult to hunt in an ice age. The spring and autumn are particularly awkward times for the hunter, because he cannot move over the slushy snow, while there is no evidence that the Neanderthalers knew of snowshoes or skis to help him cover the hard snow.

Around the caves, which were the winter shelters of people of the time, have been found the remains not merely of large mammals, such as cave bears, ibex, rhinoceros, and the like, but of many smaller animals as well, suggesting that Neanderthaler was pressed for food and would eat anything. This is just where the importance of cooking came in, because one of the tasks of a good cook is to make supplies go further.

Evidence suggests that the Neanderthalers had evolved quite sophisticated cooking techniques. They were able to keep alive members of the group who were apparently either very elderly or lifelong invalids. The remains of one young man found near La Chapelle-aux-Saints in France were those of a cripple who could have been of no use in hunting for the group. Another skeleton was that of an old man who had his teeth worn down to such an extent that he would have found it impossible to chew meat. There was no milk in those days, the food on which, in later times, old toothless people were kept alive. It seems at least likely that people of this sort were nourished on a diet of soup. Now the invention of soup making opened the door for all kinds of other sophisticated cookery.

NEANDERTHAL COOKING

What went on in the Neanderthal kitchen is a matter for conjecture, but one sensible suggestion is that he boiled animals in their skins. The hide of a flayed animal would be suspended on forked sticks, filled with meat and water, and a fire lighted beneath it. After some time the water would boil, the meat would be cooked, and the broth could then be eaten by invalids. The skin would not catch fire with the heat because it would be cooked by the water. The experiment of boiling water in a bag made of fairly thick paper demonstrates that this kind of cooking is a practical idea. There can be no doubt that cooking in a skin took place in many parts of the world, and it was still being done in Ireland as late as the sixteenth century. Old cooking habits often die hard. So do old eating habits. Until recently, Icelanders used to steam their bread in the boiling water of the hot springs by simply wrapping it in some waterproof substance and then dangling it in the hot spring at the end of a rope. Thus while the Neanderthals ate snails during prehistoric times, a whole nation of people were still eating snails in North Africa in very much later times.

Another way in which Neanderthal extended his list of recipes was by using hot stones. The hot-stone technique meant the invention of frying. In addition, stones, heated to great heat on a campfire, could be transferred to any receptacle filled with water. A sufficiency of hot stones would induce the water to boil. Anthropologists have doubted the feasibility of primitive man's being able to pick the hot stones out of the fire, just as some have doubted the possibility of cooking in a skin.

Once more observation of later cultures supplies the answer. Two stout poles, tied together at the end with a thong, provide a pair of tongs with which even the hottest objects can be removed from a fire. This was the technique used by gun founders in Southeast Asia to remove pieces of slag from a furnace.

EFFECTS OF THE DISCOVERY OF COOKING

Few discoveries have had such far-reaching consequences as the invention of cooking. Instead of spending the greater part of the day champing and grinding away at meat, which was either overroasted or raw, man could now sit down to what John Ruskin called "something nice to eat." The consequences of the discovery of cooking were not merely gastronomic. "The introduction of cooking," wrote the great American anthropologist Carleton Coon, "may well have been a decisive factor in leading man from a primarily animal existence into one that was more fully human."

Nor was the invention of cooking merely a means of acquiring increased leisure. The cooking pot became man's first laboratory, and in it he was to make all sorts of discoveries. One of these was apparently made in the age that was to follow, the discovery of poison for arrowheads. The existence of arrow poison has been inferred from gouged grooves cut into the points of bone arrowheads. Even nowadays, primitive people, such as the Bushmen of the Kalahari, make up arrow poison by cooking various ingredients in a pot over a fire.

Other discoveries made in the kitchen or around the campfire lay well in the future. Glass was invented, according to Phiny, when some Phoenician sailors lighted a fire on the beach. The beach was covered with silica sand, and the sailors propped up their cauldron on blocks of soda, which were part of the cargo. The heat of the fire fused the soda and silica into the transparent substance we know today. Man discovered how to work tortoise shell and how to polish it when he cooked a turtle in its shell. The heat of the fire softened the hard plates of the shell so that they could be easily molded, while the greasy hands of the cooks showed up the beautiful markings of the shell when they removed it from the fire. The fat was the ideal medium for polishing the material.

HOMO SAPIENS AND HIS HUNTING METHODS

It is a pity to have to announce the sudden demise of the real founder of cooking. Neanderthal man suddenly disappeared, simply wiped out by a new breed of man *Homo sapiens*. There can be no doubt why one group exterminated the other. The newcomers wanted their food supply, the game animals which were already in short supply. It was history's first, but certainly not the last, war over subsistence.

Homo sapiens means "intelligent man," and these new people *were* intelligent, perhaps too much so for their own good. Intelligence helped them to increase food supplies in several ways. The brain/power of the Neanderthals and the animals which they ate must have been about equally balanced. The Old Stone Age hunters were more than a match for their quarry. They devised all sorts of ingenious weapons for catching their prey, such as harpoons, (a spear with a barb), fish gorges, bows and arrows, spear throwers, (a sort of extension of the arm which would enable a spear to be thrown further), pit traps, dead falls, balas, and arrow poison, already mentioned.

These devices, and more tightly coordinated hunting techniques, must have considerably increased food supplies. The group was now so well regimented that it thought nothing of dismembering and carrying away the remains of a mammoth. It was able to encircle great quantities of animals and drive them over the cliff in a massacre of game. Unfortunately, this wastefulness in hunting was to become characteristic of man's attitude toward his food supplies. At Solutré, in France, a cliff used by the ancient hunters to massacre stampeding game overhangs a vast accumulation of bones estimated to contain the remains of more than 100,000 horses. Even allowing for the vast time period of the Old Stone Age, it seems obvious that these ancient hunters were wastefully killing more game than was necessary.

HIS DIET

Besides devising new techniques for slaughtering animals, the hunters extended their range of foods in a really astonishing way. They ate hackberries, cherries, hazelnuts, beech mast, wild pulses, onions, garlic, and fungi. Nothing came amiss to the table; shellfish from sea or river, land snails, or grubs, all were eaten. Nobody could accuse the ancient hunter of being fastidious about his food. In that respect he was much more intelligent than some of this successors thousands of years later, who would starve to death amidst supplies of rice, because they were only used to eating millet, or refuse to touch maize or potatoes because they had never tried them before.

Man's new adaptiveness can be seen from his invention of art as a by-product of cooking. Using the materials he got from the kitchen — animal fats, blood, and albumen from eggs — he now constructed pigments with which he painted the animals he killed. These paintings, in which the mineral ochers on the floor of the caves are worked together with cooking residues, have kept their colors undimmed for millennia in the dark recesses of the caves where they were painted. It is only the advent of modern electric lighting, and the flashes from photographers' cameras, that are at last causing them to fade.

Unfortunately for himself, man's very cleverness in procuring food by new means had now created on entirely new phenomenon, a worldwide shortage of food. The increased food supply which the original Old Stone Age groups enjoyed, groups which were extended families of, say, six couples and their children, had now caused a population explosion, causing those groups to expand to a point where they were unproductive.

INSECURITY OF HUNTING

In the best of times, hunting was a precarious way of living. The hunter had to range over an immense amount of territory, perhaps as much as twenty square kilometers (twelve and a half square miles), just to find enough game to kill. The more the group grew, the larger the area the hunters had to cover to find food for them. By about 10,000 years ago the hunting and food-gathering population of the world had exhausted its supplies of game. There was no means whereby they could increase food supplies just by hunting, yet how else were they to get a living? All over the world different peoples found the answer to that question almost simultaneously, as they turned from hunting and food gathering to becoming food growers.

2.

The Farming Revolution

ARRIVAL OF CEREALS

We noticed in the previous chapter that hunting man did not disdain to make full use of vegetable sources of diet, wherever he could find them, although so far, he grew none of them himself. One of the elements of his diet was an early form of wheat. In France, an ancient hunter even carved a picture of this plant on a bone slab which is supposed to have been a lunar calendar. The picture was a reminder that at a certain time of the year, the self-sown wheat would be ripe and ready for picking.

Though the amount of wild wheat growing in France would not yield a great deal of nourishment, this was not true of every part of the world. There was one area where wild cereals grew so abundantly that whole groups of people began to settle down there, not as yet abandoning hunting altogether, but dovetailing their hunting activities with the collection of the seeds of the wild grain.

The existence of these wild crops of wheat and barley in the fertile triangle formed between the Aegean, Caspian, and Red Seas was a real dispensation of providence for starving humanity. The wild cereals had not grown there during the Age of Glaciers because the climate had been too cold and moist to suit them, but now the climate had adjusted to their needs, and they were to be found everywhere in the area where the dryness had not become excessive and produced deserts.

There were some drawbacks about all this free food waiting to be harvested. As soon as the plants reached maturity, the ears exploded, scattering the grains (the only part of the plant that was edible) far and wide so that it was impossible to collect them. The heads were small, but on the other hand they were twice as nutritious as those of domesticated grain. Another drawback about wild wheat was that it was indigestible if eaten raw — unlike, for example, fungi, which are extremely nutritious and need no cooking.

PROBLEMS POSED BY FARMING

Grain eating, rather than meat eating, posed so many problems that by the time he had successfully dealt with them all, man had changed from a rather primitive hunter to a civilized being. The first problem he tackled was that of the bursting grain. Obviously this could be solved if he could cut off the heads of wheat soon enough to secure the contents while they were still ripe. To do this he invented the sickle, a curved piece of wood or bone, with razor-sharp flakes of flint set along the inner edge. With this tool, which may have been originally the halved jawbone of some large animal, with the teeth in place, the early harvesters were able to get around the field before the ears burst open. Everyone helped getting in the grain, children as well as woman, and in the three weeks' harvest period the Neolithic (or New Stone Age) community could harvest enough grain to allow themselves a pound of wheat or barley apiece for every day in the year.

Because of the short period of ripeness of the ears, it was necessary to be already camped beside the wild wheat fields when they became white to harvest. Soon, instead of migrating to the wild fields, the Neolithic farmers began to form permanent settlements beside them. Such settlements, man's first permanent homes, gave added advantages. The new farmers could keep on eye on the growing crop, and drive off predators in the shape of birds, animals, or rival groups of humans who might try to help themselves to the wheat. The farming community was also in a position to carry out continuous magical rituals during the period of ripening and harvest.

The ancient hunters had performed elaborate rites to ensure that they were provided with enough food by the Lord of the Game. The new farmers now evolved rituals of their own. Even nowadays in England the straw from the last sheaf of harvest is plaited into a Corn-Dolly, the symbol of the Harvest Spirit — or perhaps of a real human being who was sacrificed to ensure a good harvest.

DOMESTICATION OF ANIMALS

Permanent encampments interfered very much with the task of hunting, and as a result the domestication of animals began. This was not so great a change from hunting as one might imagine. Many hunters had kept part of their captured prey alive for a time, so as to ensure constant supplies of fresh meat. A fawn that had refused to leave the dead body of its mother, for example, would have its hoofs pared to the quick to prevent it running away, and would then be fed with cut grass till it was fat enough to be worth killing.

The Neolithic farmer began *stock rearing* with small and docile animals such as the sheep and pig, and then extended his range. The new farmers successfully tamed many animals that would be considered untamable nowadays, such as the antelope, deer, and hyena. A more likely case for domestication was the wolf, whose natural loyalty to the pack was successfully retrained into loyalty to his human master.

THE DOG

As one moves from west to east the wolves become smaller, and it is supposedly with a Syrian wolf that the first successful experiments in domestication were made. One of the descendants of the Syrian wolf was discovered in the form of the Star Carr dog from near Scarborough, Yorkshire, in England, a dog that died about 7500 B.C. Apart from the teeth of some dogs brought with them from Asia by the Indians to North America, the Star Carr dog is almost the oldest dog to be discovered anywhere. Its remains, and particularly its jaw and teeth, show that the dog was really halfway between a dog and a wolf.

Completely domesticated or not, the Star Carr dog was obviously very useful to its captors. It would eat up the scraps that would otherwise have made life in the settlement very unhealthy. Dogs can digest the toughest bones and other scraps that humans could never eat. An English surgeon, Sir Astley Paston Cooper (1768 – 1841) proved this by writing the names of famous medical men on pieces of bone in acid-resistant paint, and then feeding them to dogs, which were killed after some weeks. The action of the dog's digestion had eaten away the outside of the bone, leaving the names standing up in relief. Because penned-up dogs and hyenas would eat any kind of scraps, it did not require a great deal of effort to feed them. The Star Carr dog had in fact been badly undernourished.

Dogs, like other animals could also be used for transport, and indeed they were still pulling Eskimo sleds well into the twentieth century, when, alas, they were replaced by skimobiles. Domesticated dogs could be used for hunting, such as the capture of more members of the species, by keeping a female tethered near a trap.

They were also invaluable as watchdogs. More than one settlement has been saved by the barking of dogs giving the alarm of an evening's approach or the outbreak of fire. In much later times, cackling geese warned Romans that Gauls were trying to capture their citadel.

The biggest advantage about a domestic animal (other than dogs) however, was the fact that it was a readymade supply of fresh meat. It could be slaughtered when the resources of the settlement were low. The flesh of domesticated animals was much tenderer than wild game. The wild animals were often killed as the result of a long chase, during which all the glycogen in their bloodstream had been used up.

Even nowadays, all kinds of domestic animals end a long life of service to mankind in the slaughterhouse. I bought a garlic sausage in Boulogne recently and was enjoying it very much. I happened to read the label: "*Viande asinine.*" The sausage was donkey meat. The horses, ponies, and donkeys, over which the English enthuse so much while they are still up to their work, are, at the end of their working lives, shipped across the Channel to the *boucherie chevaline*, or horse butcher, which is a feature of all large French towns.

The aurochs, or wild cattle, eventually became transformed into domesticated cattle, and gave milk as well as meat. They could also be employed for plowing. Pigs were very useful as an addition to the food supply, but like dogs they were almost equally useful in cleaning up the rubbish heaped about the settlement before it could breed flies and disease. Many thousands of years later, during the 1830's, hogs were still doing all the street cleaning in New York.

FARMING METHODS

The penning up of domestic animals produced not merely dung, which was the only manure that Neolithic folk knew, but the prolonged pasturing of animals, particularly goats, would tend to reduce the

number of weeds and also to do something to break up the hard surface
of the ground.

It was on the small enclosures produced by penning, rather than on
large farms, that more intensive agriculture now began. Noticing that
some patches of corn produced larger ears than others, the early farmers
began to select some of the large-eared grain to use as seed corn in
gardens on the penned-up soil. To break up the ground even further, they
used an ingenious instrument called a digging stick, which was a pointed
wooden stake, its point hardened in the fire, weighted by a stone bored in
the middle, with the stick passing through the hole.

On the soft tilth thus produced, manured perhaps by further penning,
the farmer would let his seeds fall, scattering them broadcast, confident
that, if the spring rain fell in sufficient quanitity, they would produce a
good crop for the following summer.

So farming, rather than just food cropping, became the Neolithic way
of life.

Instead of being a wandering hunter, man had now become a settled
member of a community, living in the same place, growing the same
crops, einkorn and emmercorn and their variants, year after year.

SOIL EXHAUSTION

This was the trouble. Growing the same crop year after year in the
same field soon took the heart out of the land, in spite of fertilizing. Not
every farmer added ferlilizier to his soil, be it noted. India, where the
new Neolithic farming methods were soon to produce one of the first and
most brilliant of the early civilizations, at Mohenjo Daro, is notably a
country where dung has never gone into the soil to enrich it. It has mostly
been used as fuel.

The land on which the new farmers grew their crops was virgin soil,
that is, it had never been farmed before. You can grow bumper crops on
virgin soil for about ten years (as American farmers were to discover in
the Middle West), and then a decline sets in. The crop does not disappear
altogether, but it diminishes to much that the farmer may well feel that
the work he puts in no longer yields its due reward.

SLASH-AND-BURN-CULTIVATION

Puzzled and disturbed at their declining yields, and certain that
somehow they had offended the Spirit of the harvest, the Neolithic
farmers moved away from their exhausted fields. When they came to

virgin forest, they would begin to cut down the trees and brushwood with stone axes. This not so difficult as it sounds. Recently three Danish archaeologists found that they could clear 600 square yards of birch forest in four hours, using flint or obsidian ax blades. More than a hundred trees were felled with a single Neolithic ax blade, a blade which had not been sharpened for more than 4,000 years.

When the farmers had cut down all the trees and undergrowth, they would pile them up, leave them to dry, then set fire to them. The conflagration would clear the ground and also enrich the soil with ashes. Farming would then begin, with the result that the whole process would repeat itself. So the change to a grain diet had very considerable consequences for mankind. The destruction of forests meant the loss of the animals and birds which had once found shelter in them. As the trees disappeared, the climate altered for the worse and became much drier and hotter. The rains, no longer impeded by tree roots, leached the goodness of the soil down into the rivers, and frequently the soil itself followed.

Barren, denuded lands now hastened the process which the slash-and-burn cultivation methods of the new farmers had begun. The new farming peoples began to fan out from their original home in the Fertile Triangle, moving at considerable speed, taking the new ideas of agriculture with them all over the European and Asiatic continents.

So fast did the slashing and burning go on that special mines had to be sunk to dig up the flints needed for ax blades. There, far below the surface, industry began as miners pecked away at the chalk faces, armed with picks made from deer antlers. Heaping up the knobbly flints in baskets, they would then carry them up the shaft to the surface, climbing tall ladders. On the surface they would be "knapped" into shape in ax factories.

POPULATION EXPLOSION

The Neolithic farmers were pushed along by another big population explosion. Between 7,000 and 4,000 years ago, world population went up from three million to over a hundred million, and it was all due to the Farming Revolution. The Revolution had allowed the emergence of a settled way of life and regular supplies of good food. Life had become much safer, women had become more fertile. For the time being, there was enough for all. Yet it was obvious that such a state of things would not last forever. By about 5000 B.C. the Neolithic settlers had begun their great trek out from the Neolithic heartland of the Middle East, where conditions had been just right for the cereals they grew, and for their domesticated animals, all of which were native to the area. By about 2000 B.C. the Neolithics had reached what was, for them, the limits of the known world. Penetrating westward into Europe and Scandinavia, southward into Africa, and north and east into Russia, they had come to the natural limits of their kind of farming in the deserts of the south and east, the Arctic tundra in the north and the Atlantic Ocean in the west.

Having carried out this great migration, which on the whole had been a very peaceable one, with hunting and farming folk integrating well, the Neolithics found themselves back where they started. They were tied to the fields where the yield was bound to decline, and this time there was no chance of expanding outward any more.

The Farming Revolution had produced irrevocable change. The old forests, which had held the game, were destroyed, and the game with them. In Denmark, for example, where the slash-and-burn farmers had arrived about 2500 B.C. the primeval forest of huge elms, ashes, oaks, and limes had disappeared. New types of forest now appeared, including many birches. Weeds moved in, including plantain and rye, a weed which was eventually to be utilized as a food crop. Finally, after the farmers had left to look for new fields, a forest of large trees reasserted itself, but it was a sterile forest compared with that which had sheltered the wild aurochs, giant elks, bison, and bears. These were now either extinct or had been driven over the horizon.

Trapped on declining farms, with little game but with an increasing population, the Neolithic folk were to lose the peaceful qualities which had characterized them in their great dispersion.

They could not increase production, because they used an inefficient system of cultivation, in which their plows merely stirred up the top of the soil but did not bite into it. They could cultivate the light topsoils, but not the heavy valley bottoms which are a feature of mountainous Europe. Neolithic Europe and Asia now formed an analogy to a lobster pot that has been sunk to the bottom of the sea, and which has succeeded in catching a number of lobsters, some large, some small. The piece of rotten fish tied to the bottom of the pot which constituted that bait has now been devoured by the lobsters. They cannot get out, so what are they going to eat next? The answer is: each other. An era of battles now heralded the approach of a new age which was going to end the period of peaceful farming. Helped on by a new discovery, how to melt bronze, there now began the Era of Continuous Warfare, which has lasted in Europe (with short breaks) between the Neolithic and modern times.

CEREAL PROCESSING

Let us first glance at how Neolithic man grappled with the quite considerable problems posed by moving to different kinds of foods from those eaten by the ancient hunters.

The wild cereals, whose distribution area overlapped in the Fertile Triangle, all had one thing in common. Their grains were extremely indigestible. Could some method be found to process the wild wheat and barley and in particular to separate the grain or seed part from its undesirable package — tough bran and abrasive outer coasting of chaff, plus the spiky ears of "awn" or beard in which it was wrapped?

Various ingenious processes were carried out by Neolithic man to get to the edible part of cereals. He boiled the heads of grain in water, in pits heated by dropping red-hot stones in them. The heads of corn became soft enough for the grain to be separated from the chaff and awn just by rubbing with the fingers. The softened individual grains were picked out by the fingers and eaten immediately. Further boiling of the grains in water would turn them into a soft and delcious pudding which medieval folk called frumenty. It has now disappeared, but as late as the eighteenth century it was one of those snacks which could be bought in London streets.

A much more popular process than boiling was threshing the corn to free the wheat from the chaff. The ears of corn were beaten with a hand-held flail, or an ox trampled round and round on the hard surface of the threshing floor on which to ears of corn were being pounded. The wind, or large winnowing fans, blew away the light chaff, leaving only the heavier grain, with a lot of bran still adhering to it.

A further step carried on the extraction process and also preserved the ears of grain almost indefinitely. The wheat or barley would be swept off the threshing floor to one side. Large fires of wood would now be lighted on the stone or baked brick threshing floor till they had burned down to white embers. The embers would then be raked away, and the ears of corn thrown onto the floor. The heat split the chaff, detached the awn, and roasted the grain. Depending on the amount of heat that the grain was exposed to, it would be either parched or toasted or popped like popcorn.

When this heating-up process had been completed, the fibrous parts of the wheat or barley would then be blown away. The grain, thus roasted, would keep almost indefinitely. To eat it, all that needed to be done was to powder it by hammering it and then make it into porridge by adding water.

Hammering the grain was at first carried out in a mortar, or stone bowl, with a stone hammer. Wooden mortars and pestles are still in use in Africa for powdering various foods, such as peanuts. Mortars, either in stone or wood, had undoubtedly been in use before Neolithic times for grinding up nuts such as beechnuts.

The next important piece of processing machinery to be invented was the *quern*. Querns were flat, shallow troughs of stone which were rubbed with a flatter stone small enough to be held in the hand. The quern need not be made of stone; there were many pottery ones. Years ago, in a deserted village site in Malawi, I picked up a baked pottery quern hand stone. Friction between the two stones or pottery bricks at top and bottom reduced the hard parched grains into meal. In the more elaborate querns the grinder sat astride the ''saddle'' quern and pushed the stone back and forth, straining the back muscles and rending the air with the noise of the two stones screeching against one another. Querning was terribly hard work, always done by females. Throughout history there is only one record of a woman having escaped from her task of querning the corn.

In the middle of the third century A.D., Cormac Mac Airt, high king of Ireland, raided Britain and carried off a Pictish princess. Cormac's queen became jealous of the beautiful prisioner and ordered that, like other slaves, she should grind a certain amount of meal every day. The Pictish princess was unable to fulfill this obligation because she was now pregnant. Thereupon Cormac sent to Britain ''for an artificer who could construct a mill.'' This was evidently one of the new water mills, which could grind grain by revolving two circular millstones, which were operated by means of a mill wheel, turned by the force of water. The meal was ground, and so the queen's injunctions had been obeyed.

Roasted corn was one of the great culinary inventions. It was still in use in Tibet until the Chinese Communist invasion, in the form of *tsampa* or roasted barley corns ground into meal. It would keep indefinitely, and could be prepared by adding cold or hot water to it. Homer's heroes even add barley meal to wine. It could be mixed with other foods, such as broths, and was so light that it could easily be carried about. Husked grain, whether parched or toasted or not, became the great food of antiquity.

BAKING

As travellers, hunters, sailors, and soldiers lived almost exclusively on gruel or porridge, it is not surprising that among one of these groups, gathered around a campfire (even sailors would tie up for the night and go ashore to cook their food) baking was discovered.

A little stiff porridge, dropped onto a campfire stone which had been made really hot by the fire, turned into a cake if left long enough. Homemade bread usually requires a lot of that mastication which, said Count Rumford, acts "very powerfully in promoting digestion."

The Neolithic Age had begun as an era of porridge and gruel, composed of mixtures which included seeds and nuts as well as ordinary cereals. A human sacrifice who had been strangled and thrown into a bog at Tolund in Denmark contained in his stomach a porridge made from a variety of ingredients.

BREWING

Watery gruel left in a jar, or perhaps grains of barley which escaped being parched and sprouted, may have led to the other great discovery of the Neolithic Age, brewing. Beer can be made from most cereals, and in Neolithic times it was probably very like the thick and porridgy African beers, on which many African (males) seem to live without bothering to take any solid food. The desire to eat something fermented is apparently a perfectly natural one, not an acquired taste. The Eskimos, who have no fermented liquors, eat rancid fat for the same reason that we drink beer, wine, or spirits. Beer was certainly more palatable than newly drawn water, which was often charged with sediment that had to settle before the water was drunk. It was also more convenient to have a store of jars of beer ready to hand than to send someone to the river to fetch a drink. Many places where water is drawn were the haunt of crocodiles or wild beasts. Beer was such a success that Neolithic man soon experimented with other fermented drinks, such as mead, made from honey, and wine.

Wine making may have begun when a jar full of fruit juice was accidentally left to ferment. Or else it may have resulted from an attempt to make a fermented grape juice sauce, such as the verjuice which was much used in medieval times. It apparently began in the mountainous region of northern Mesopotamia, Syria, and Palestine, where vines grow wild. Soon vinestocks were being transplanted from the sterile hilly ground on which they grew naturally to fertile soil which might have been used to much better advantage in growing food.

Unlike beer, wine does not quench the thirst. The percentage of alcohol which it contains is much greater than that in beer, and it encourages the drinker to eat, and drink more. So wine has always been very good business for the restaurateur; and some kinds of cookery, such as the classical French cuisine, promote greater wine drinking by adding too much salt and grease to the food. As the wildfowler Colonel Peter Hawker pointed out as early as the nineteenth century, the ideal drink with thirst-provoking French cookery is not wine at all, but some kind of fizzy drink, such as the aerated mineral waters which had begun to appear at that time.

LAW OF OVERCONSUMPTION

One of the problems of wine, from the point of view of dietetic history, is that it suffers from what one might term the *law of overconsumption*, which seems to overtake all drinks in history. The early drinkers never drank their wine unmixed. They added large quantities of water, usually hot water, because cold drinks are a very modern taste. If you called for drafts of pure wine, as did one Gallic chieftain, this could be a sign that you intended to commit suicide, as he did. Nowadays nobody adds water to wine except the French and Italians, very sober people on the whole.

It is noteworthy that many nations, such as the Japanese and the Chinese, have managed to get through history with a lot less alcohol than people in the West. Even nowadays, a Japanese cup for rice wine is a mere thimbleful. If you want a larger drink, you either have to empty your cup many times, or call for a tea cup, thus revealing that you are a debauchee.

Even in Neolithic times, cups for drinking wine were fairly large, although, as I have said, the wine was mixed with a lot of water. Tea, coffee, and chocolate, when they appear, are also to be affected by the law of overconsumption. Tea in Japan or China is a pale, straw-colored liquid; in England it is so dark that you cannot see the bottom of the cup.

The large amounts of cereals which Neolithic folk ate must have made them extremely costive. It also ruined their teeth. Anyone who could afford to eat bread regularly would be likely to outlive his teeth. They would be ground down, right to the gums, by the large quanitities of pulverized stone which entered the flour from the quern. Most Neolithic folk must have suffered acute agonies from toothache.

SALT

Salt had become a necessity in the human diet during the era of the ancient hunters. Now the need for salt brought about a flourishing salt trade. Salt was so universally in demand that special trading routes were developed just to distribute it. It became a currency which commanded universal respect.

Cattle were so important that they could not be killed just to provide meat, while they could still have been giving milk and used as transport animals. So most meat in the Neolithic diet was probably associated with temple sacrifices. Fortunately the gods were content with the offal of the beasts sacrificed to them, so worshippers at the Neolithic shrines, such as that at Catal Hinjuk, in Turkey, would be able to join in the feast that followed the sacrifice. Though most Neolithic deities were not so much animal gods as those connected with the soil — various Earth Mother goddesses — images of animals seem to have played a large part in worship, particularly bulls and cows.

EGYPT

It is now time to glance at two favored countries, which enjoyed a yearly surplus of food, and whose food production never declined. One of these countries was Egypt, where along the valley of the Nile the river rose once a year between July and September, swollen by the floods that had fallen as rain on Central Africa. For a time Egypt turned into a sea, but it was a sea of riches, because when the waters receded, they left behind them a thick coating of slimy mud, full of dissolved vegetable matter from the rivers, lakes, and forest of Equatorial Africa. This mud was a natural fertilizer which renewed the vitality of the soil of Egypt. For thousands of years, down to our own day in fact, it has produced bountiful crops several times a year, without any artificial fertilizer being added.

So there was no need for the Egyptians to move away in search of fertile fields, as other Neolithic folk did. On the contrary, they knew that they must remain near to their beloved river, because, as the Greek historian Herodotus put it, ''Egypt is the gift of the Nile.''

As the floods receded from the land, the Egyptians came down from their stiltlike houses, plowing in the quickly drying alluvial mud with their wooden plows drawn by oxen. All the old weeds had been killed by the flood. Those which now came up were quickly dealt with by a small number of laborers.

The farmer now sowed the fields with his first crop, barley, wheat, or flax. In the gardens by the river grew beans, scallions, onions, and cucumbers. Long-horned cattle pulled the plow or in season dragged loads of juicy grapes to the wine presses. Donkeys carried loads of corn to the granaries or storehouses which existed up and down the country. Ducks and geese cackled in the yards around the houses, ready to supply the national dish of old Egypt, roast goose, washed down by beer. Herds of sheep and goats made the most of the pasture where the cultivated land met the desert, where all life ceased.

The settled surplus the Nile paid as a dividend to the Egyptian farmer had made the inhabitants of the Nile Valley rich, individually as well as nationally. Several more crops could be raised than in famous "Crete of the thrice-sowed fields." One peasant could produce enough food to keep himself, his wife, and his family three times over. Apart from weeding and irrigating with the *shadouf*, a primitive crane for lifting water from the river into the irrigation ditches, there was little work to be done in the fields between November and April, when the harvest began.

The richness of Egypt was observable not merely in the peasant's well-stocked vegetable clearing, his vines heavy with grapes, and the date palms bowed with fruit that shaded his little house, but in the great monuments which covered the land. These represented the work of innumerable specialist craftsmen and artists, paid out of the national surplus.

Even in the Neolithic world as a whole the leisure produced by agriculture had enabled men to carry on pursuits other than those immediately concerned with food. There were spinners, weavers, basketmakers, potters, stone and wood carvers, traders and priests.

In Egypt all these categories could be very considerably enlarged. The national surplus of agriculture allowed all sorts of people to develop their own personal service to the community. The actual task of sharing out the food surplus was divided between the priesthood, which owned an enormous part of the whole country, and the Pharaoh, the spiritual as well as the temporal ruler of the Egyptians. The strong rule of an autocratic Pharaoh had come about in part because of the necessity of controlling food production. For example, someone had to give the signal for the breaking in of the irrigation ditches when the Nile had reached its highest point. All agricultural activities had to be coordinated, and only one person, vested with the highest authority, could achieve this. The Pharaoh dealt successfully with all kinds of problems which were to baffle later monarchs and governments. He ensured that the Nile brought its yearly gift but did not overflow where its silt would bring no benefit, by carrying out enormous flood-control and irrigation works. During the slack time of the year he dealt with the problem of temporary unemployment, and kept the work force in good heart and muscle (conditions which can only be achieved by constant hard work) by having them build for him the most sumptuous edifices ever conceived, pylons, colossi, temples, and particularly tombs, which were invaluable in keeping the whole work force of Egypt in constant employment during the slack time in the agricultural year.

The Greek historian Herodotus was shown over the greatest of all tombs, whether in Egypt or anywhere else, by a native Egyptian guide. The guide translated for his benefit an inscription carved on the outside of the pyramid which has long since disappeared. The inscription recorded the incredible amount of radishes, onions, scallions. and other food consumed by the laborers who had built the pyramid.

The specialist workers mentioned a paragraph or two which helped Pharaoh prepare the statistical material on which his rule was based. There were scribes, civil servants, astronomers, scientists, doctors, architects, and agronomists. One Pharaoh was even prepared to accept the assurance of a young Hebrew predictor that there was going to be famine and made ready to meet it. Though they were a deeply religious people, the Egyptians certainly did not believe that everything would always turn out right in the end and that we lived in the best of all possible worlds. They had carefully studied the Nile, and they knew from experience that it sometimes failed to cover the cultivated land with an inundation for as long as seven years together.

Such a catastrophe would have meant famine and cannibalism. Later, during the years of Arab rule, medieval Egyptain chronicles record that Egyptians trapped one another and feasted on each other's flesh during times of food shortage.

In the days of the Pharaohs, however, a fall in the level of the Nile, which registered on the Nilometer at Rhoda, was simply a signal to open the storehouses, where the taxes of years ago — bushel after bushel of parched corn — were distributed to the hungry populace. There can be no doubt that Joseph, and his predecessors and successors, managed the business of famine relief much more successfully than did that other comptroller of famine, Sir Charles Edward Trevelyan, who allowed a million Irish to die during the great Potato Famine of 1846 – 47. The ancient Egyptians were able to make an agricultural civilization work, which can be seen in the enormous investment they made in buildings and land reclamation. Yet they possessed several advantages which no other country ever enjoyed. Until the latter part of Egyptian history they remained completely isolated from the rest of the world. They had no neighbors warlike enough to cross the Sinai Peninsula to invade them; they had no desire to dispose of their surplus grain for export, because they had no exports. Above all, all classes in Egypt were prepared to bow to authority and do as they were ordered by Pharaoh.

DIETARY RESTRICTIONS

During the palmy days of Egyptain civilization, the only Semites with whom the inhabitants of the Nile Valley made contact had been peaceful nomands, such as Joseph and his brothers, and their descendants. Young Moses, who had been brought up at the Priest's School at Philae, had certainly absorbed the wisdom of the Egyptains, but he must also have learned by their example to do otherwise. Extremely rigid food taboos governed the subjects of Pharaoh. They were forbidden to eat certain foods and never to eat in the presence of a foreigner. Joseph withdrew when he entertained his brothers at his home for the first time. This refusal to eat with strangers reflects the arrogance of the Egyptains. Conscious of their own lofty culture, they refused to acknowledge that there could be any virtue in anything that was not Egyptain. By comparison, Moses' injunctions about food were light indeed.

MESOPOTAMIA

The miracle of the Nile had only been repeated in one other part of the world, Mesopotamia. It will come as a surprise to no one to learn that it was here, where the two rivers, Tigris and Euphrates, discharged their silt on fields which would later yield abundant crops, that the other great civilization of the Farming Revolution began. All the agricultural and culinary trimphs of the Egyptians were repeated, more or less, in the lands between the two rivers. Cheese, butter, and buttermilk enriched the palate and the outline of the wealthy Mesopotamian. The great gardens of Babylonia, some of them raised on terraces, harbored many of the vegetables which were later to become staples of the Western kitchen, like the carrot and fennel. Though the river fish were not equal to those of Egypt, there were plenty of birds to be caught in the marshes between the rivers. Long-tailed sheep proclaimed the riches of Babylon. Vines grew abundantly, but only for the rich, and by Assyrian times as much as 40 percent the arable land had to be taken up in cultivating the grain for the beer drunk by the poor.

Unlike the Hebrews, the Assyrians were Semites of an extremely aggressive and warlike breed. The new inventions which accompanied their military prowess, the chariot and bronze weapons, were already fanning out like dragon's breath far beyond their immediate sphere of influence. In 663 B.C. the Assyrians determined to solve their food production problems by adding yet another country to their empire. They captured Thebes, and the brilliant development of Egyptain civilization came to an end.

3.

The Merchandizing Revolution

TRADE IN FOOD

The aspect of food history which has suggested the title of this chapter is the export of food. There had been some exports of comestibles during the Farming Revolution, but not to any great extent. The Egyptians who could afford it had drunk Cretan wines, imported in the local Mycenaean pottery. Though there were plenty of good Egyptian wines, what is exotic and imported has always a charm, or why else should Americans, with their own splendid wines, bother to import wine from Europe?

For many countries, however, food imports had become not a matter of customer's choice, but an affair of necessity. On Crete itself, an island which had once produced trees large enough to make beams to span the palace of King Minos, at Knossos, there were now no sizable trees to be seen at all. What had happened on Crete had, by and large, happened all over the Middle East and the eastern Mediterranean. New invaders, armed with the bronze weapons which had emerged from that center of war, the Middle East, had swept down on the mainland and islands of Greece. They had stripped the forests with the new bronze double axes which were among their principal weapons. By the beginning of the seventh century B.C. the populations of the new invading stock had outstripped its resources. From the tops of the once leafy mountains, the torrential rains of the Aegean winter cascaded down the deeply grooved valleys. They tumbled along with them into the sea the soil of the hillsides which, clothed with trees, might have supported great herds of swine to feed the growing population. For unlike the Jews or the Egyptians, the Greeks had no abhorrence of the hog.

THE OLIVE

One reason for the denudation of the countryside was the appearance of the tree which now almost alone represents the vanished forests of Greece. The olive strikes deep roots into the crevices in the exposed rocks of the hillside, where the soil has been washed away, sponging up all the moisture that might have promoted the growth of other trees. The olive was an agricultural triumph. It had taken great persistence and ingenuity to turn the spindly, thorny bush that once grew wild in Syria and Palestine into a great tree with glaucous leaves and waxy berries. It had also required great ingenuity to tame the wild mouflon into a domesticated goat. In both cases the result was not quite what was required for the setting. Both were masterpieces, but misapplied to the eastern Mediterranean. The long roots of the olive and the long teeth of the goat, nibbling into the very surface of the land, now left nothing to show of the Homeric forests which had once waved over Greece.

Olives are delicious when eaten raw, or pickled in brine. They also yield an oil rich in calories capable of enhancing the driest hunk of bread. Unfortunately, olive oil was the only illuminant known to the ancients other than candles and torches. Olive oil burned in every home in receptacles ranging from the earthenware lamp of the philosopher Epictetus (he had substituted a pottery lamp for the iron one which had been stolen, so as not to tempt passersby) to the great silver candelabra of King Antiochus of Syria, which the Roman proconsul Verres stole for his own use. Olive oil greased the limbs of the Greek as he issued from his bath and kept his muscles supple in the gymnasium. It produced the principal fuel which burned his dead body on his funeral pyre, and was poured on his ashes in the form of perfume.

No wonder there was not enough oil to eat in Greece, but even if there had been enough oil, there was no longer enough barley bread to pour it on. Though the Greeks tried to eke out their bread with dried fruits and tunny fish, it was obvious enough, by about 600 B.C., that there was not enough fertile land left in the peninsula to grow barley, and hardly any land at all suitable for raising cattle.

GREEK WINES

In an attempt to stop the food catastrophe, the Greeks started to export themselves to found colonies overseas, while they also imported foreign food in return for their own luxury exports. These luxuries included the Greek olive oil, which was of high quality, and Greek wines, which had the finest reputation of any in the Mediterranean. These valuable vintages were exported in what we would consider to be very unsuitable containers. Glass bottles were only made in very small sizes, while the wooden barrel had not yet been invented by the Gauls in France, so the Greeks used pottery containers for their wines from Chios and Lesbos. These pottery containers were known as *amphorae* (singular: *amphora*), and they were gigantic man-size jars with two lugs but no flat bottom. Their pointed base had to be thrust into soft sand, or into a specially made rack.

Amphorae must have been very difficult to carry when full of wine. One has been found in the Roman fort at Qasr Ibrim, in Nubia, which got broken before it could be opened. This must have happened often.

Corks are an invention of the Middle Ages. They are cut from the bark of the cork oak in Portugal. Before corks were invented, amphorae were plugged with a stopper made of pottery, packed around with a rag and secured with pitch. These stoppers did not always do their job very efficiently, and an amphora of wine would be likely to arrive in Italy from its homeland in Greece, tasting both of the seawater that had seeped in around the stopper and also of the bitumen that had melted off the end of the stopper into the wine.

FOOD ADDITIVES

It is amazing how soon food additives became an acquired taste. Because consignments of rice were held up to one Chinese city, and arrived tasting very musty, the rice consumers of this particular town acquired a taste for musty rice and insisted on having it thereafter. In a similar way, customers for Greek wine soon began to demand additives. The wine merchants obligingly added salt water or turpentine to the shipment to give it the right flavor. The resinated taste of much Greek wine, still noticeable today, is due to the resin-treated goat wineskins in which much of it was stored.

In an attempt to secure for their needy citizens the daily porridge and barley bread which were their staple fare, the leaders of Greek city-states now gave them Horace Greeley's advice: "Go west, young man." Westward lay many countries where the Farming Revolution had not spent its full effect. Many of the people in *Hesperia*, as the Greeks called the West, had not evolved an elaborate agricultural civilization, or were not agriculturists at all but pastoralists. These simple shepherds were prepared to come to an agreement with the Greeks and allow them to occupy part of their land in return for the exports they had to offer, particularly wine. The inhabitants of Gaul, where the Greeks founded one of their most flourishing colonies, Massilia or Marseilles, did not have a single vinestock growing in the whole of what is now France. They were beer drinkers and were eager to obtain the wine that the Greeks had to sell, so eager in fact that they would willingly exchange a slave for an amphora of wine.

COLONIZATION BEGINS

And so the process of *colonization* began, something which was to become a permanent feature of European life until our own day. The spot which the Greeks were most eager to colonize was Italy, particularly southern Italy and Sicily. These countries were named by the Greeks "Big Greece," not without reason, because they both became thoroughly Grecized. Even nowadays the inhabitants of Naples look much more like Greeks that the general concept of what an Italian ought to look like. What made Magna Graecia so attractive was its potential as grain-growing country. Great plains, almost unknown in Greece, seemed to lie waiting for the plowman with his ox team.

THE BATTLE FOR WHEAT

The descent of the Greeks on Naples and Sicily heralded the beginning of a great international struggle for grain, a struggle that was to end only when a strong power, Rome, became dominant over the others, securing world rule on the unspoken mandate that there should be an abundant supply of grain for the nations of Europe and that it should be allowed to move freely.

Like the international struggle for oil going on in our own time, which the Battle for Wheat very much resembles, it took a long time to move into its final phase, and there were many side issues. The conflict began among three of the principally concerned countries, who attacked a fourth.

Just north of Magna Graecia were the colonies formed by the Etruscans, a people who, if their own traditions could be believed, had been forced out of Lydia in Asia Minor to find food elsewhere. A picturesque legend connected with this emigration was that famine had been so severe in Lydia that the Etruscans ate only on alternate days, and on the fasting days they had invented board games to while away the time and allay the pangs of hunger. The Etruscans were one of the powers now menacing the wheat-producing center of the world, Magna Graecia.

To the south, in North Africa, lay Carthage. The Carthaginians were colonists, too, like the Greeks of Magna Graecia. They had left their original homeland in Tyre in Phoenicia to settle on the North African coast. It was not their hunger but their business acumen which had induced them to settle there. Like Sicily and southern Italy, North Africa was one of the natural granaries of the Mediterranean. They wanted to control the great harvests of North Africa, but at the same time to corner those of Sicily and Italy, so that they could monopolize the whole market.

Carthage, Etruria, and the states of Old Greece such as Athens now became immersed in a series of wars to control the wheatlands of Magna Graecia. In the end it was none of these warring nations but a new, emerging country called Rome that was going to secure the prize. The Romans needed grain more than any of the other nations mentioned, because Italy is a very mountainous country, with few plains. The hill farms of the Romans were already well adapted for growing the other crops planted there, but they needed the wheat of the south to feed their vast armies.

THE ROMAN ARMY'S DEPENDENCE ON WHEAT

By the time of the Roman Republic grain had become the sinews of war, as petroleum is with us today. Immense stocks of food were needed for ancient warfare. A siege, such as that of Eryx in Sicily, might go on for years. Both sides needed to be continuously provisioned during the siege, and in practice the only kind of food that could be stored to supply them was grain. Grain was easily available almost everywhere, it could be stored in bulk, and could keep in different climates, and it could be made into various kinds of dishes. Meat, on the other hand, as the Roman cookery writer Apicius points out, will only keep two days in summer without being cooked or salted. To be without grain was the greatest misfortune that could overtake a Roman army. "The army," writes the Roman general Julius Caesar, "was in great difficulties over the supplies of grain, to such a degree that for some days together the soldiers were without wheat and drove cattle in from the distant villages and so held out against great hunger. Nonetheless there were no complaints from the men." Obviously Caesar regarded an army without wheat as one that was virtually starving. Why did they not eat something else?

One reason was that the range of foods was extremely limited. Like their opponents, the Romans ate vegetables when they were available (they introduced the chickpea, olive, fig, and rice to Germany). Vegetables, and the other snacks that Romans liked, such as cheese and bacon, as well as fresh meat, were not always available nor always very appetizing. It must be remembered that cattle were not yet bred to provide delicious beefsteaks. They were used as draft animals, they were skinny and tough, and they were considered so precious that it was only by indulging in the fiction that all meat meals originated from a sacrifice to the gods that the Romans could persuade themselves to eat meat at all. A Gaulish cow was probably no treat to the hungry legionnaires of Caesar, there was probably as much horn and hair and bone about the cow as there was meat.

Cattle, too, were often diseased, and this was why the soothsayers of Roman and Greek religion professed to be able to predict the future from the character of the internal organs of sacrificed beasts. Obviously cows, sheep, and pigs with beautifully clean and normal organs would not have provided all the differences of appearance on which sacrificing priests relied to make their auguries.

Bread was a different affair. The Roman legionary had been eating bread all his life. Even as a civilian he had lived almost exclusively on bread and olives. The legionary would of course be eager to vary his diet. He would eat meat if one of the officers had gone out hunting, or if some enemy cattle had been captured. He might well add beans, lentils, fruit, or rather exceptionally fish or oysters to the meal, but the main course would be bread. He would be given three pounds of grain per day, which he would grind in a handmill which was shared by each group of soldiers.

This flour was then made into hardtack or *buccellatum* or baked into proper bread. When the Emperor Caracalla was leading the life of an ordinary soldier, he "ate the bread that was available, and with his own hands ground his personal ration of corn, making it into a loaf, which he baked in the ashes of the campfire and ate." All over Europe soldiers were doing the same as the Emperor. Even outside the Roman Empire proper, in places like Germany and Sweden, barbarians who had done their time with the legionary eagles could be seen baking their bread in the prescribed fashion, watched no doubt by admiring groups of friends and relatives who would afterward be persuaded to sample a piece.

Occasionally Roman soldiers would try something else other than bread, for variety. They were always writing home, and their letters were full of requests for presents of food. Out of sixty letters from Roman soldiers found at a place called Wadi Fawkhir in Egypt, all but a very few are requests for food. Yet if they did not get their ration of wheat during the campaigning season, and while they were resting in winter quarters, in the form of bread, porridge, or pasta, they would have been unable either to fight or work — and they worked all the time they were not fighting.

The only exception was soldiers in disgrace. Men who had broken in the face of the enemy were given barley instead of wheat, as a punishment. It was a much more effective punishment for cowardice in the field than simply executing every tenth man (as the French did in World War I). It went on for years, and everyone could see the unfortunate soldiers as they ate their meal of shame.

FOOD AND STATUS

For some reason status is very closely connected with food. In the 1840's many of the starving Irish would not go into soup kitchens and walk out carrying food; they had their pride. Starving English men and women would not eat black bread, because that was what the French ate. Nor would they eat soup — the French also ate soup. Nor did they wish to eat oatmeal — that was eaten by the Scots.

PROBLEMS OF CORN SUPPLY

The task of feeding a Roman army was an enormous one. When the Roman General Agricola became governor of Britain, in A.D. 78 – 84, he stocked up every fort in the island with enough grain to last a year.

Each Roman soldier would eat about a third of a ton of grain every year, and this amount would occupy half a cubic yard in the granary. If each soldier received three pounds of grain a day, and the frontier forces of Britain in the third century numbered 25,000, then the daily consumption of grain would be three and a half tons. Though some of this was requisitioned locally, or even grown on military land, around the fort, most of it would have had to come from a Roman supply depot somewhere. Grain was so precious that a permanent Roman camp or fort was full of specially built granaries, well-designed and constructed buildings, which had ample ventilation and were as fireproof, ratproof, and insectproof as Roman architects and builders could make them.

As Rome's military might expanded, so did her need for more grain. Julius Caesar had only once nearly faced defeat in the field, and this was in Gaul, where a brilliant Gaulish leader, Vercingetorix, realized that his countrymen could defeat the Romans if only they could prevent them from raising supplies of grain from the occupied countryside, or moving it up from bases in Roman territory. Vercingetorix's plan did not succeed, but Caesar remembered the crisis he had faced. In order to obtain constant supplies of the universal food of soldiers (it could be fed to their horses as well) he invaded Egypt during the Roman Civil War. Egypt, like Sicily, was a great granary.

THE GRAIN SHIPS

In the future Rome was going to draw the bulk of her grain supplies from Egypt. They arrived in Ostia, the port of Rome, in specialized bulk carriers such as the *Isis*. This grain ship was a fully decked vessel with enormous holds, four in all, of great carrying capacity. She had a length of 180 feet, a beam of 50 feet, and a hold 44 feet deep. The stern post of the *Isis* was formed of the head of the sacred Roman goose (the bird whose cackling had once saved the citadel). At the stem a statue of the goddess Isis, an Egyptian deity, symbolized the grain-producing wealth of Egypt.

The *Isis* was merely one of a fleet of grain carriers, which left Egypt every harvest time and after a brief stop at the Piraeus, the port of Athens, proceeded to Ostia. A fleet of galleys, stationed at Misenum (near Naples), did nothing but patrol the seas during the sailing of the grain fleet to ensure that supplies arrived in time. If the fleet was only briefly delayed by bad weather, there was panic in the city.

ROME — A GRAIN EMPIRE

Egypt was only one of the grain-producing countries which Rome had acquired to feed her armies. The Roman armies had marched from one grain-growing country to another. When they stopped to take in some country that was not notable for wheat production, such as Greece, there was some special reason for it. Greece has a rugged coastline with innumerable islands, and during the Republican period, the Greek archipelago had been a lurking place for pirate ships, such as the dreaded pirate fleet of Cilicia. It had seemed essential to the Romans to subdue Greece completely for the security of the grain fleets. Gaul and Britain were particularly useful acquisitions to the list of grain-producing countries. When Roman arms came to the limit of the effective wheat-growing areas, the German forests and the deserts of the Middle East, they simply stopped.

Unfortunately for the Romans, the grain frontier on which they had decided to halt their advance was a very untenable line. By overrunning the settled, agricultural countries, which they would have been better advised to leave as neutral buffer states, they now found themselves faced with aggressive semicivilized peoples such as the Germans in the north and the Parthians in the east, neighbors who were a perpetual thorn in their flesh. Even in Britain, it would have been more sensible for the Romans to halt before they were face to face with the wild Caledonians, a people who were only excluded from the settled south by means of the greatest fortification built in the Roman Empire — the Hadrian and Antonine walls.

BREAD AND CIRCUSES

A new burden had now been laid on the Roman exchequer. It had assumed the task of feeding not merely the army, but virtually the whole of the city of Rome.

Distributions of free food to the Roman people had begun in Republican times. Attempts had been made to cut back these gifts, but without much success. Julius Caesar congratulated himself because he had cut the dole queue back to 150,000 adult male citizens, but he apparently started the custom of giving free meat and oil as well as grain. By the time of his immediate successor, there were 320,000 regular recipients of state food.

Annonae distributions were a charity for the rich. It was not the really impoverished Roman who was being fed — there would have been some sense in that — but the Roman citizen. The presents were a bribe to make the Romans forget they had lost their former political power and were now living under an autocratic emperor. From every point of view except the economic one, the bribes system was a very successful one.

In the gladiatorial amphitheater Romans would be given a packed luncheon basket called a *sportula*, which contained bread, oil, pork, and sometimes wine as well. There would be enough for the several meals that could be eaten during a day's amusement at the amphitheater, with enough to take home to the family afterward. "Rome," said the satirist Juvenal, "is governed by bread and circuses."

Without directly causing the fall of the Roman empire, the grain drain contributed to the general imbalance which now began to afflict the later Empire.

Enormous armies garrisoned the grain-producing countries, such as Britain, but they had to be fed. The Roman garrison in Britain consumed 1,277.5 tons of grain every year, but their requirements were really twice that amount, because the aim of every commander was to have at least a year's supply in hand, in case of emergencies. The garrison must have been consuming a large proportion of the grain it was supposed to be securing for Rome.

Because grain supplies came from the ends of the earth (so far as the Romans were concerned), they were very much in hazard. Grain coming from Egypt or North Africa had to travel right across the Roman Empire to get to Rome itself. A storm, the revolt of a province, the invasion of some barbarians, could throw the whole system into confusion.

So, too, could the refusal or late payment of taxes, because the grain that the Roman soldier and civilian ate was not commandeered by the government — it was bought by the taxes paid by the provincials. A more agriculturally minded civilization might have tried to cut the Gordian knot by intensifying wheat production at home. Mussolini tried to do this in the 1930's, with some success. The Romans, however, wanted their home farms to grow some of the expensive luxuries for the table, which will presently be described.

EASTERN

It is no surprise to learn that when the barbarian invasions began in earnest in the fifth century A.D. the Western half of the empire collapsed very quickly, while the Eastern half, based on Byzantium, survived very nearly until Columbus set sail for America. So long did the Byzantine Empire, Rome in the east, linger on that the last titular Byzantine emperor, Ferdinand Paleologos, lies buried in North America, in the churchyard of St. John's, Barbados.

The reason for the survival of Byzantium is not hard to seek. It could depend on the abundant harvests of the Middle East, still producing wheat in spite of centuries of cultivation, while the Western hemisphere swiftly lost the great wheat-producing areas of Britain, North Africa, and Egypt.

The outflow of grain was not the immediate cause of the destruction of Rome. That was brought about by what one French historian has called the "hemorrhage of gold."

GOLD GOES EAST

Financial crisis was what marked the end of the Empire — a financial crisis that saw the Emperors unable to raise the armies they required, because of the sheer shortage of cash. This had been caused by the *annonae* system. The later emperors had to take very drastic measures to maintain the distribution of bread, such as compelling bakers to become a hereditary caste and forcing them to sell bread at the prices the emperor dictated. If the bakers tried to escape from their jobs, they were thrown to the wild beasts in the arena.

These measures were undertaken so that the citizens of Rome could eat their packed lunches while criticizing the courage and skill of gladiators battling for their lives. Yet even these harsh measures had been unavailing, and right at the end of the Empire the free distribution of food had to be abandoned, because there was no money left to keep it up.

The Romans had no truck with paper money or credit payments. They always settled their accounts in bullion or copper coin. Unfortunately for Rome, bullion had been getting scarcer and scarcer as the centuries wore on, and even the copper as well as the silver coinage of the Empire now began to show marked signs of debasement. Where were the gold and silver going? As we will see, they were traveling east, to be used for payments to buy the delicacies that had now become characteristic of the upper classes.

Quite simple meals had sufficed for the Greeks. They were concerned about their figures, because they were vain, but they were also prepared to go to considerable lengths to keep fit, because to the Greek, regular exercise was part of the way of life of every gentleman. Self-restraint was the principal classical Greek virtue, the others being justice, wisdom, and courage.

THE ETRUSCANS

The Romans had inherited a tradition of fine food and fancy eating from their predecessors, the Etruscans (who had also introduced them to the cruel gladatorial games of the amphitheater). To step into an Etruscan tomb, such as those which honeycomb the center of Italy in Umbria, is to descend to a perpetual banquet. On the walls of the tombs the Etruscans are portrayed, just as they were in life, raising the wine cup, helping themselves to the delicacies before them, or listening to the music of the performers, who kept up a perpetual accompaniment to each pleasure of the Etruscan day and particularly to the feast.

The Etruscans had studied to eat well; unfortunately many of them ate too well, and the phrase *obesus Etruscus*, or "the fat Etruscan," became a byword in Rome. Many of the Etruscans are portrayed on the terracotta statues that covered their sarcophagi or tomb chests as very fat people indeed. Did they overeat themselves out of history? It's possible.

THE ROMAN FEAST

Though the early Romans affected to despise the Etruscan indulgence in food, their descendants eventually outdid them. It must be remembered that in Republic times Roman society was emphatically a male one. Roman ladies lived in a sort of haremlike seclusion and did not join their husbands when the latter met for a dinner party. Hence the grace and restraint that women have always been able to impart to meals were markedly absent in early Roman times. (During the later days of the Empire this prohibition was rescinded, but by then the pattern of self-indulgence seems to have been set.) With no ladies present, except for professional singers and dancers, there was nothing to attract the admiration of the diners except the decoration of the room, the wine, and the food. The Romans really let themselves go. Their motto might have been "Eat, drink, and be merry, for tomorrow we die," and just to emphasize this theme, a silver model of a skeleton, or a mummy, was always brought in at Roman dinners and exhibited to the company, as a reminder to them to enjoy the good things of this world while they could.

Dinner was the one occasion during the day when a Roman aristocrat could relax. He would have risen long before dawn, without breakfast, to meet his political supporters or clients. Lunch might or might not have followed some time during the day, as he went to the law courts or the Senate House. There is a Latin word, *impransus*, which means "having gone without lunch."

Late afternoon would have been spent in the baths, where there was not merely the enjoyment of a Turkish bath, but usually a game of handball afterward. On the way from the baths the young Roman might have picked up one of those professional diners-out who were called "parasites." The parasite was a professional guest. In return for a free meal he would retell the news and gossip of the day (there were no newspapers), tell several amusing stories, and be prepared to laugh at his host's jokes.

By a rather late hour in the evening, the Roman would arrive at a friend's house, nicely relaxed after a day divided between business duties and social obligations. A relaxed mood was suitable for enjoying a chat about the events of the day with a small number of intimate friends, not less than five and not more than nine. "More than the Graces, and less than the Muses," was how the Romans described the right number of guests for a dinner party.

Politics was taboo as a subject of conversation. The Emperors were extremely suspicious of the Roman aristocracy, whom they saw as the natural leaders of any revolt against them in an attempt to reintroduce the Republic. A great deal of the conversation was about food and wine.

The guests met in a special dining room of the house, set aside for just this purpose, warmed in winter by a hypocaust, or central heating unit built under the floor. The room was usually either decorated with painted frescoes or ornamented with panels of brilliantly polished marble. It was "carpeted" with a mosaic made from countless little cubes of brightly colored stone or glass. One of the most famous patterns for floor mosaic, which is mentioned in literature as well as present in actual remains, was an "unswept floor." This looked like a plain floor with, lying upon it, all the objects that one would expect to drop to the floor during a dinner party: peach stones, crumbs of bread, nuts, bones, the shells of shellfish, even a mouse which had come out to eat the crumbs! This mosaic might not deceive anyone today, especially as the mouse is drawn as though lying on its side, but it may have looked much more deceiving under torchlight. At any rate it must have served as a splendid conversational piece.

Heavy jokes of this sort seem to have part of the Roman routine at dinner. In a romance by Petronius, the arbiter of fashion and expert on wine and cookery under the Emperor Nero, there is a reference to a roast sow which is opened up by the carver — only to allow "dozens of thrushes to come whirring out."

While the guests looked admiringly around the room, praising the host's taste in furniture and decorations, the serious business of the dinner would begin. Someone would be selected by the host to decide in what proportions the wine and water would be mixed. As the light of the candles began to be reflected from the glittering mica scattered with minium and sweet-smelling saffron on the floor, slaves would come around with chaplets of flowers which they would place on the heads of the guests. The diners would settle themselves on their couches, for Greeks, Romans, and Etruscans reclined on couches while they ate instead of sitting on chairs. The couches, like the dinner tables, would be of citron wood, cedar, silver, or, costliest of all, the tortoise shell which had been introduced to Rome by the great giver of dinners, Pollio. The drinking cups, at first plain gold or silver, and later bullion studded with gems after the manner of the barbarians, would be raised in the first toast, to the genius of the Emperor, and then the guests would reach out for the first course, or rather the first appetizers, olives imported from North Africa.

To such a pitch had gastronomy been carried at Rome that the experienced diner-out could tell, blindfolded, whether the olive he was eating had been picked with the bare hand, or by someone wearing a glove, and also where it had come from. The first course might include sausages, of which the Romans were inordinately fond, flavored with Indian pepper, pepper which had made an eleven-months' voyage to Rome. There would also be Syrian plums, mixed with pomegranate seeds, which had come from the Near East.

EXOTIC DISHES

Though some of the dishes would be home-grown ones, such as lettuce or asparagus or radishes, they might well be garnished with imported salt pickle from Byzantium. There would certainly be oysters accompanying this course — not Italian ones, they were too commonplace, but probably oysters from the Locrine Rocks in Greece or from far-off Britain. The Romans had a genius for transporting live creatures from the ends of the earth. If they could bring in live ostriches from North Africa and crocodiles from Egypt to Rome, then they would have no difficulty in procuring fresh oysters from Britain. Figpeckers (a kind of bird) cased in a pastry egg might figure among the hors d'oeuvres.

As the banquet wore on, the exotic nature of the imported delicacies being served to the guests became much more apparent. Thus though the wine might be Italian (it was much more likely to be from Chios, a Greek island), it would be sweetened with Greek honey, which had come from Mount Hymettus. The game course (ring doves, field fares [thrushes], capons, ducks, and hare) might be of local origin, but the fish sauce with which the birds were dressed was certainly not. This sauce, called *garum*, was made from a small fish called the scomber, and it came from Leptis Magna, one of those beautiful Roman cities whose ruins are still standing in North Africa. Roman cooks were inordinately fond of this sauce, and it would already have featured in earlier courses, along with a mysterious lost herb, called "silphium" which was presumably imported. Every Roman regarded himself as an authority to some degree on gastronomy. Even Saint Jerome, a very austere Father of the Church, gives instructions somewhere for cooking a partridge.

After the game course came fish, such as mullet and turbot. The Romans were very fond of fish, and the Emperor Domitian even called the Senate together to discuss how best to cook a gigantic turbot that had been presented to him.

THE FIRST COOKBOOK

No doubt, after this imperial request, the senators hurried home to consult their cooks, and they in turn began to unroll their copies of the best-known Roman cookbook, by Apicius.

Apicius' book may not have been written by M. Gavius Apicius,* but it is certainly the kind of book he might have written. Isidorus mentions him as the author, and also states that his was the first cookbook ever written. Seneca tells us that, after having spent a hundred million sesterces on food, Apicius suddenly found he had only ten million sesterces left. Faced with the prospect of starvation, he killed himself.

Unfortunately for Domitian's senators, there is no recipe for cooking

*Apparently there were two persons named Apicius, both authorities on cooking. The first of them lived under Augustus and Tiberius, the second under Trajan. The second is the more celebrated, and it is he who invented the cakes named for him. He ran a college of gastronomy in Rome, which was open to the public. He spent two and a half million in satisfying his love of fine fare, and wrote a book in which he showed how to stimulate the appetite, *De gulae irritamentis* ("Incentives to gluttony"). Pliny calls him "The great abyss of prodigals."

turbot in Apicius, but there is plenty of information about how to cook other fish, and especially what sauce should go with them. Apicius' fish sauces contain Indian pepper, Syrian sumac, Jericho dates, Chinese coriander and cassia, Welsh onion, Persian sugar, Parthian assafetida, Sinhalese cinnamon, Indonesian mace, nutmeg and cloves, and Malaysian cardamom.

The last courses would do nothing to diminish the notion that a Roman dinner was a sort of international charivari, in which those ingredients which cost the most and which had come from farthest afield were most favored. The Umbrian boar from Italy would be served up with Syrian and Egyptian dates, while the pastries and sweetmeats that brought dinner to a close had been sweetened with Indian sugar, dried fruit from the Tarim Basin (in Turkestan) and Madagascar, and almonds from Anatolia.

Just to prepare a dinner for six, the host had to send all over the known world, an extent of some eight thousand miles east and west, and spend enormous sums of gold and silver to satisfy the producers of these costly delicacies. He had not grudged the trouble and expense partly because he knew that people would talk about his open-handed hospitality, partly because of the determined singlemindedness that the Romans applied to everything, even giving dinners. The Roman idea was to be *tenax propositi* ("firm of purpose") — once you have made up your mind to do something, go through with it and, if possible, do it better than anyone else.

ROMAN GOURMETS

Whether it is true that Apicius really killed himself because he feared to starve on nearly four million dollars a year or that one Roman gourmet trained himself to eat meat that was hotter than anyone else could bear, so he was always able to get the best cuts before his fellow guests, it is certainly true that the fashionable Roman was a great gourmand and a great spender on the pleasures of the table.

The people who lavished fortunes on their dinners were not all fashionable exquisites by any means. Lucius Licinius Lucullus was famous for his victories on sea and land and his rule in North Africa. Yet Lucullus spent over $90,000 on a dinner for just three people, Pompey, Cicero, and himself. Once when he happened to be dining alone, an unusual occurrence, he noticed that the menu seemed rather dull. "Give the cook orders to prepare a dinner in our usual style," he told his steward. "Tonight Lucullus dines with Lucullus." No wonder "Lucullan" has entered the language as an adjective for elegant dining.

THE PEPPER ROUTE TO THE EAST

To get the oriental delicacies demanded by the stylish hosts of Rome, Romans now sailed eastward. The hardy seafarers of the Empire had pioneered the most extraordinary adventure in ancient history, the sea route to India. Starting from Arsinoe, an Egyptian port near Suez in Egypt, they sailed down the east coast of Egypt, around the southwestern corner of Arabia at Aden, thence along the southern Arabian and Persian coasts till they reached Barbaricum, the first Indian port. The name merely means "port of the foreigners."

It was not till A.D, 45 that a Roman sailor called Hippalus discovered that there was no need to follow this coast-hugging route. It was possible to sail directly from Aden, to India, blown by the southwest monsoon of summer, then load up with Indian sugar, pepper, and spices, wait till winter when the monsoon shifted to the opposite quarter, and sail back on a northeast wind.

It was at least fifteen hundred miles from Aden to Barbaricum with no landfalls on the way except the island of Sokotra. Hippalus and his fellow Roman navigators had no compass or sextant, but the skies of the East are much clearer than those in Europe and provide good navigation by the stars.

Everyone was eager to follow the example which Hippalus had set, because, although the open-sea route entailed three thousand miles of sailing out of sight of land, it was a shorter route (thus increasing the profits) and also much safer. Out at sea a Roman captain might hope to avoid an encounter with the dreaded East African pirates, men whose tall African stature made them seem like giants to the short and stocky Romans. A cohort of archers was often carried aboard merchant ships to ward off pirate attacks, thus putting up the price of spices even more.

Because only one ship out of two made the return voyage safely, merchants felt justified in asking the most enormous prices for their products. Pliny remarked: "No year passes in which India does not impoverish us of fifty million sesterces, and does not furnish us with merchandise, which is sold amongst us for a hundred times that amount."

The trouble about importing spices was that they all had to be paid for, and there were only two commodities which India would accept in return. One was wine. Romans exported wine to India in amphorae, although they were already using barrels for shipping drinks for shorter distances along rivers. The sheer weight of the amphorae aboard must have helped send many Roman ships to the bottom. Altogether Rome shipped so much wine to India that the price of wine went up in Italy, but it was not enough.

To settle the balance of payments, Rome had to send abroad gold and silver. Gold has always occupied a very special place in Indian life. It is a paradox that, although so many of the inhabitants of the great subcontinent are desperately poor, much of the gold supply of the world has disappeared into India for good. In India gold turns into temple treasures and marriage ornaments, both sacred objects which cannot be liquidated.

FOOD IMPORTS CAUSE AN ECONOMIC CRISIS

Gradually, under the strain of the outflow of gold to India, an economic crisis set in, in Rome. It was signaled by the fact that the richest people in the Empire, the Emperors, suddenly found that they could not meet their obligations, either to pay for free distributions of food or, more important, to pay their armies.

Unable to support the armies, which alone could have stopped the barbarian incursions, the Roman Empire simply collapsed.

4.

The Medieval Kitchen

REACTION AGAINST GLUTTONY

One fairly predictable reaction to the fall of the Roman Empire was a swing away from the luxurious life led by rich Romans. The fall of Rome was attributed by the early Christians to its excesses, and although the Fathers of the Church tended to dwell on sexual excesses, we have already seen that excess at the dinner table really did have a great deal to do with the collapse of the Western world.

As a reaction to the gluttony and wine bibbing which had characterized the Roman Empire at its height, the hermits and anchorites of Egypt ate barely enough to keep themselves alive.

> The chief and pattern of all the recluses [wrote Lord Curzon], was the great St. Macarius of Alexandria. . . . Self-denial and abstinence were their great occupations, and it is related that a traveler having given St. Macarius a bunch of grapes, he sent it to another brother, who sent it to a third, and at last, the grapes having passed through the hands of some hundreds of hermits, came back to St. Macarius, who rejoiced at such a proof of the abstinence of his brethren, but refused to eat of it himself. . . . During Lent, St. Macarius fasted all day, and sometimes ate nothing for two or three days together; on Sundays, however, he indulged

in a raw cabbage-leaf, and in short, set such an example of abstinence and self-restraint to the numerous anchorites of the desert, that the fame of his austerities gained him many admirers.

EUROPEAN MONASTICISM

Self-mortification on Saint Macarius' model might do very well for the Desert Fathers, compelled by the burning sun of the desert to make as little exertion as possible, but a handful of beans would not enable any religious, no matter how enthusiastic, to support the cold of European winters. It was left for an Italian, Saint Benedict, to hammer out a monastic rule that would combine that needs of everyday humanity with the spiritual potentialities of Eastern monasticism. Benedict of Nursia drew up this rule about 530 at Monte Cassino in Italy, still standing despite repeated assaults, the most recent the Allied bombing of World War II.

The essence of the rule of Saint Benedict was its humanity. It did not order the monks to fast right through the year, as did the rule of Saint Basil, which is still in force for Greek monks. It prescribed a sufficiency of food, frugal but adequate. It even allowed the monk a daily draft of wine.

Saint Benedict's tempering of Eastern asceticism with the needs of ordinary men did not destroy the spirituality of the Benedictines, but increased their productivity very much. Saint Benedict had always been concerned with productivity. *Laborare est orare*, he had written, "To work is to pray." Needless to say, he meant work performed for the glory of God, not for individual gain.

The Benedictines certainly lived up to their motto. Every Benedictine monastery was a hive of industry, in which agriculture and industry flourished. Nor were art and literature forgotten. In the *scriptorium*, or writing studio, the calligraphers labored to copy and illuminate books. On sheets of parchment — themselves the product of Benedictine industry because they were made from the hides of the monastery herds — they carefully preserved every Latin manuscript on which they could lay their hands.

So although the pepper fleets had ceased their voyages between Egypt and Barbaricum, and a Latin work such as *The Periplus of the Erythrean Sea*, which gave sailing directions for the voyage to India, merely appeared an antiquarian curiosity to the monks, the day would come when some scholar would blow the dust off this book. When he had read it, would he too not wish to visit the lands where the pepper tree grew?

THE TASTE FOR BREAD

One final effect of the fall of the Roman Empire must be noticed, because so far it has escaped the notice of the historians of food. With the disruption of normal trade, wheat exports to the north, which must have been considerable, at one time ceased altogether. The glamour cast by Rome had, as has already been noticed, given the barbarians a taste for Roman food, and particularly for bread. Even people who had resolutely remained outside the bounds of the Empire had nonetheless become regular bread eaters. The English were an example. The word "lady" meant, in Old English, "the person who gives out the bread."

In Scandinavia, people had also become bread eaters, but now they had nothing with which to still the craving. Wheat, from which Roman bread was made, is very demanding in its soil requirements. On land that is infertile, sandy, or badly drained, wheat yields only precarious and scanty crops.

Arable land is very scarce in Scandinavia, except in Denmark, and much of that was subject to flooding. Because crops of wheat could not be raised, the Scandinavians grew rye instead. The trouble with rye was that you could not make bread from *pure* rye. Even nowadays, what is called "rye bread" by bakers is made from a mixture of rye and wheat flour, with the latter predominating. Dark leavened rye bread was not introduced into Scandinavia till the Middle Ages, when it arrived from Mecklenburg and Pomerania. And rye crackers, thin crisp wafers, was only invented in the nineteenth century.

So the only kind of bread the Norsemen could make was barley bread. They had not discovered how to leaven it, and it had to be eaten straight from the griddle pan on which it was baked, while it was hot. If allowed to cool, it became hard as a stone and just about as digestible. Barley bread was, then, for house consumption only. You could not store it or take it with you into the fields to plow or out in a boat while you were fishing. As only barley bread could be produced by the stony fields of the North, they were sown year after year with barley. No other crop ripened in the short Nordic summer, and the constant repetition of the same crop, in the scanty acreage available, quickly produced on impoverishment of the soil that resulted in smaller and smaller crops. In a desperate attempt to eke out the barley, Scandinavians added to the bread mixture the ground-up inner layer of pine bark. This was a protection against scurvy, but as Eric Oxenstierna wrote in his recent study of Norse culture, it was so bitter and indigestible that, for those who have not eaten bark from childhood, it is almost inedible.

Of the two samples of calcined bread which have come down to us from old Scandinavia, one contains pine bark and ground dried peas, the other is barley mixed with a good deal of grit or stone dust from a hand mortar. "In the barren north," writes Oxenstierna, "We have a history of extreme poverty that lasted until 1870, which is why we are so well versed in these pitiful food customs."

VALHALLA

By contrast with reality, in poetry and legend the Norsemen could dream of feasting on all sorts of delicacies — including bread. In a poem of the Viking Age, "The Lay of Rig," "loaves of thin light bread, made of wheat" are served up to the hero by his princely host. It seems fair to assume that the poet who composed the poem had never eaten wheaten bread himself. Nor had he partaken of the most delicious of meals that the Norsemen could conceive, because that was served only to brave warriors who had ended their fight in the Hall of the Dead, or Valhalla. They were picked out for this honor by the "Choosers of the Slain" or Valkyries, who fetched their heroes' spirits to Valhalla from the field of battle on the cruppers of their horses. The warriors then spent enernity in feasting and drinking beer from great horns handed to them by the tall and beautiful Valkyries.

Roast pork was also provided for the heroes. A divine hog called Saetherimni allowed itself to be killed and roasted (some say boiled) every day. After it had been eaten it obligingly came to life again to provide tomorrow's meal. Nothing is said about bread in Valhalla, but no doubt you could help yourself to as much as you wanted.

There could be no doubt that Valhalla offered a very cheerful contrast to the real Scandinavia, where there was no wine whatsoever, because there were no vines, little beer (because if you had not enough barley to make bread, then it would be an obvious absurdity to brew beer), no pork, boiled or roast, but only (in famine years) seaweed, bark, and lichen.

THE HUNGRY VIKINGS OVERRUN EUROPE

Still, if Valhalla was a long way away, there were places of abundance nearer, Western Europe and, in particular, England.

It was no light undertaking to sail to England, or anywhere else, in a Viking ship. Such vessels averaged seventy-one feet long, were fitted with movable deck planks, had a very shallow draft and a very low stern which could easily by pooped by a following sea. A good gale could pile up an entire Viking fleet on the rocks, as happened once at Swanage, in England.

The Norsemen, or rather Vikings as we must now call them (that was the Norse name for someone who set off on a piratical expedition), felt that all these dangers were less to be feared than that of starving to death on their own farms. So in 793 they made their first successful raid on England, attacking the rich and defenseless monastery of Lindisfarne.

It was those countries that were least able to defend themselves against the Vikings which were most affected by the widespread raiding that followed. In Russia, a Viking named Rurik formed the state of Kiev, around which Russia was to grow. In the north of France and Germany, dragon-headed ships rowed far up rivers to attack peaceful communities. In England they were likewise successful at first, conquering and settling the central area known as Danelaw, until at last they were checked by the man who, at his coronation, had seemed likely to be the last king of Wessex, Alfred the Great.

At one point Alfred was so hard pressed by the invaders that he was forced to take refuge in the swamps of Athelney in Somerset. There he was sheltered by a cottager, whose wife ordered him to keep an eye on the cakes of bread as they baked in the ashes of the fire (just as they had baked for the Emperor Caracalla), Alfred was so absorbed by the terrible hour of crisis in which his country stood that he forgot about the cakes, and they burned.

Athelney marked the low ebb of Alfred's fortunes. He was able to gather another army and attack the Danish king Guthrum, and the Danes, surrounded in their camp, agreed to abandon Wessex and fall back on the Danelaw. Guthrum and some of his followers offered to become Christians — a quite genuine conversion. Guthrum took the English name of Athelstan, had coinage struck in his new, baptismal name, and was doubtless pleased to learn that Christians do not have to wait till the next world to enjoy feasting. They are taught to pray for their daily bread in this.

Although the Vikings altered the whole face of Europe — founding the duchy of Normandy, for example, which was to become a fruitful mother of "Frankish" kingdoms — they had nowhere more important effects than in England.

Hitherto the English had not been noted for a desire for seafaring or traveling. Alfred was the first king to build a navy. The grafting onto England stock of the stubborn Viking strain, however, was to produce great changes in the national character.

MEDIEVAL FOOD — LEGEND AND REALITY

The American tourist who, after an afternoon spent watching the reenactment of a tournament or perhaps a display of falconry outside some medieval English castle, finishes up the day by treating himself to a "medieval dinner" may well imagine that he has seen a recreation of the part. But that saddle of brawn, quince jelly, and wine in pottery mugs does not really represent the kind of fare on which folk lived in the Middle Ages.

It is always difficult to make the past come alive again, and nowhere more than when it comes to medieval food. There had never been anything like medieval food before, and there was never to be anything like it again. Writes William Edward Mead, an expert on medieval food:

> Modern taste is so different from that of four or five hundred years ago, that scarcely one of the favourite dishes served at feasts would now be found eatable. . . . Scarcely anything was prepared in what would now be regarded as a simple and natural fashion. . . . The ideal, apparently, was that nothing should be left in its natural state, but rather devilled and hashed and highly spiced. . . . Few things are more extraordinary than the type of food our ancestors ate. . . . Much mediaeval food was chopped up small or pounded in a mortar. . . . The reason for this constant maceration is to be found in the lack of forks. There was no easy way of cutting meat upon one's plate, and hence the cutting was done by the carver.

Before you complain to the present owner of the castle that the meal you have eaten is not exactly the same that his ancestor would have served to Richard I, try preparing a medieval dish yourself, and see whether you really like it. Here is a recipe for poached eggs.

"Take eggs, break them, and seethe [boil] them in hot water. Then take flour and mix with milk and cast thereto sugar or honey and a little powdered ginger and boil all together and colour with saffron.'' (Saffron was almost the only important medieval spice to be grown in Europe; much of it was raised at Saffron Walden, in Essex.) ''And lay thy eggs in dishes and cast the broth thereon. Blanche powder is best.'' (Blanche powder is a mixture of ginger, cinnamon, and nutmeg, all of which had to be grown in the Far East and were extremely expensive. When, in a medieval recipe, spices are mentioned, the amount required is never a mere pinch, but at least a teaspoonful, perhaps more.)

SPICES

The whole of medieval cookery revolved around the use of spices. Of all the ingredients in the diet, spices were the most desired. When, for example the Venerable Bede (673 – 735), a famous English monk and scholar of the Dark Ages, was on the point of death, he carefully divided among his closest friends his greatest treasure, a handful of pepper. Even Bede, a monk, who was supposed to own no property at all, had not escaped the lure of this most desired ingredient in the medieval diet. The closer one got to poor folk, such as the humble tillers of the field who could afford no spices, the less food was flavored at all, and the nearer one got to rich men's tables, the larger grew the amounts of spices one was obliged to consume. The cost of these spices was the heaviest charge laid on the purveyor of the kitchen.

The kitchen of Jeanne d'Evreux, widow of King Charles le Bel (The Fair) of France, who ruled between 1312 and 1328, was a veritable treasurehouse of spices. It contained 3 bales of almonds, 6 pounds of pepper, 13½ pounds of cinnamon, 23½ pounds of ginger, 5 pounds of ''grains of Paradise'' or cardamom, 3½ pounds of cloves, 1½ pounds of saffron, ¼ pound of long pepper, ⅜ pound of mace, ⅛ pound of powdered cinnamon, 5 pounds of cumin, and 20 pounds of sugar in four sugar loaves.

Why on earth would anyone want to have such quantities of spices in his kitchen — spices which, moreover, had cost an immense amount of money? Well to begin with, every page of every medieval recipe calls for spices.

Venison, for example, was considered very insipid if not spiced. Boiled venison required the addition of parsley, sage, powdered pepper, cloves, mace, vinegar, and a little red wine. ''Numbles'' of venison, the edible viscera of a game animal, which has given us the phrase ''humble pie,'' needed to be prepared with wine, powdered pepper, cinnamon, powdered ginger, vinegar, and salt.

The most famous of all medieval dishes, custards and blancmange, called for an even greater use of spices. Blancmange was not a dessert like the modern dish, but meat or fish, boiled with sweetened almond milk and seasoned with sugar and salt. Medieval custards were also quite different from those of today. Here is a recipe:

> Take veal and hammer it into little pieces in a pot, before washing it out. Then take clean water and boil powdered pepper, cinnamon, cloves, mace and saffron. Add plenty of wine, and boil the powdered veal in it. Cool the broth, take the white and yolk of eggs and strain them. Add them to the broth to stiffen it. Pour it into pie cases, along with chopped dates, ginger, and verjuice [a tart sauce of grape juice or apple juice, fermented], add it to the pie cases, and bake.

Yet to say that the cookbooks called for spices is really begging the question. Other explanations for the lavish use of spices may be found in the very nature of the staples of medieval diet. Those who could afford to ate meat and fish rather than the bread and vegetables which had figured so largely in Roman diet. Olive oil, one of the Roman staples, had disappeared altogether from northern Europe. The only place in which you would have seen any oil in the North was in some great cathedral when a king was being crowned. Oil had become so precious that it was now a treasure. The Anglo-Saxon writer Aelfric notes that his fellow countrymen used butter as the Italians used oil with their food.

Wine, that great necessity of life for the people of the ancient world, had also disappeared completely from northern Europe, except from the tables of the rich, and from church, where it symbolized the blood of Christ during the Mass.

MONASTERIES, AND FOOD AND DRINK

Many monastic gardeners tried to grow enough vines to supply wine for the services of the abbey or convent church. Alexander Neckam (1157 – 1215), who wrote the first English cookbook, also wrote about gardening, and he devotes a complete chapter of this account to viticulture. William of Malmesbury says that the wine of Gloucester is hardly inferior to those of France. (This may well have been true; there has recently been a great revival of wine growing in England.)

In a continental monastery such as Saint Gall in Switzerland, the vineyards would probably cover several acres. Wine was regarded as a medicine in the Middle Ages, and there was good Scriptural authority for this. The Good Samaritan had poured wine and oil into the wounds of the poor traveler he befriended, just as Italians still do with minor cuts. Wine was also drunk as a restorative. Saint Paul urged Timothy to take a little wine for his stomach's sake. So it was logical that a monastery which cultivated medicinal plants, as did Saint Gall, should also have a vineyard.

In countries which had once been Christian but had been overrun by the Muslims, such as Egypt and Spain, the monastery vineyard played a very large part in securing good relations with the local authorities.

Officially wine, and every other alcoholic drink such as beer, was forbidden to Muslims. In practice Muslim rulers and even Caliphs sometimes felt a desire for a glass of wine. The only place where they could obtain it was in a monastery. By supplying local rulers with wine, monasteries were able to continue to survive the persecution which they had undergone from the time of the original Muslim Arab invasion down to our own day.

Thus in Egypt, one of the greatest of the Sultans, Khamarawah, son of Sultan Ahmad Ibn Tulun, used to spend hours at the monastery of Al-Kusair, rapt in admiration of the mosaics in the church, which represented the Virgin Child, attended by angels and surrounded by the twelve apostles. After admiring the beauty of the church music, he would go out with a few friends to a colonnaded verandah which he had had specially built. There with a few friends he would watch the sunset and drink the wine the monks served to their guests.

In addition to securing the survival of the vine, monasteries strove to perpetuate other food plants as well. In the small Scottish town where I grew up there had once been an enormous monastery, which was now in ruins. People with gardens had kept up a species of apple which the monks had originally grown, called "Abbot Oslin's apple." They were small but very sweet.

The monasteries were not able to secure the survival of all the Roman food habits, however. In England the Romans had introduced pheasants and Burgundian snails. The pheasants went wild, and they were eventually to feature as a very important game bird, one of those kinds of "forbidden food" which were supposed to be eaten only by the upper classes in England.

The snails also ran wild, escaping from the snail pits where they had been kept in Roman villas. Nobody has bothered to eat any of them since, and they are a quite undisturbed piece of British wildlife except for occasional collecting by the proprietors of foreign restaurants in London.

BREAD VERSUS PORRIDGE

Wheaten bread was still found in Western Europe, but only as a luxury confined to the rich. The poor tended to eat bread made from the barley, rye, and oats which grew well in a northern climate. Rye had appeared in European fields originally as a weed, but even before the fall of the Roman Empire, it had come to be grown as a field crop.

Bread making and eating had become a universal European habit, thanks to Roman example, except in very out-of-the-way countries where old habits died hard. In Bronze Age times, for example, many Europeans, such as the human sacrifice victims discovered in bogs in Denmark, had eaten porridge of various sorts. The only country where porridge eating hung on as a feature of life in medieval times was Scotland. The Scots did not make much bread, preferring to rely on oatmeal, either eaten as a porridge, or baked on a griddle as a kind of pancake. In Ireland too very old food habits persisted. Right down to the sixteenth century the Irish continued to cook the meat of slaughtered cows in their skins on an outside fire, and to drink a great deal of milk. Elsewhere in northern Europe beer drinking became almost universal. Other alcoholic drinks such as mead, made from honey, also took the place of wine, which, as has been noticed, was quite out of the reach of the ordinary individual.

SHIFTS IN FOOD PRODUCTION

One reason why post-Roman Britain no longer cultivated large crops of wheat, as they had in the past, was that life had become much more dangerous. Wolves and outlaws prowled, and the nobility were often at war. Rather than put in the enormous amount of labor needed to clear forests and plow deep, many medieval folk preferred to pasture animals instead. The inhabitants of medieval London could drive their flocks into Epping Forest to pasture during the day and then drive them back within the safety of the city walls at nightfall.

Pastured animals exploited the riches of the great forests that covered Europe. Their fats replaced the olive oil which the Roman world had used so extensively and which could no longer be imported from North

Africa (now in Arab hands). Frenchmen, Italians, and Spaniards continued to consume home-grown oil in those parts where the olive trees would grow, but in the North men learned to butter their bread.

AUTUMN SLAUGHTER OF ANIMALS

The herds of oxen and great droves of swine that fed on the beech mast and acorns of the forests, along with great flocks of geese, provided fresh meat during the summer. During the winter, however, all fresh meat disappeared, because there was not enough pasture. The little hay that could be cut had to be saved for a few essential animals — plow oxen, draft animals, breeding stocks, and the war horses of the feudal nobles and their retainers. So medieval folk became adept at preserving meat. It was dry-salted or pickled in brine or smoked like bacon (which took its name from *bucen*, the Anglo-Saxon word for "beech mast").

Slaughter of hogs began in September and continued throughout the fall, but the traditional day for slaughtering the herds of beef was Martinmas, the feast of Saint Martin of Tours, November 11. There was a great feast at which people ate up all the offal and side cuts — chitterlings, blood puddings, and tripe, which would not pack well in brine — a sort of festival of lights. This annual slaughter was called Yule in England, and the Church was eventually able to convert this wholly pagan festival into a Christian feast. By means of a little management of the calendar, it was arranged to fall about the time of Jesus' birth. Nonetheless Christmas did not altogether lose its old name, Yuletide.

Right through the winter everyone ate salt meat. Long before spring the first cases of scurvy would begin to appear, because the vitamins present in a fresh diet, notably vitamin D, would be absent from crudely preserved beef and pork. It may have been an attempt to ward off the affects of scurvy that caused verjuice to be so popular as an ingredient in meat sauces. Verjuice was made from fruit that had been allowed to ferment, either crabapples, green apples, or grapes. The verjuice would keep through the winter in a fermented state with salt added to it. It must have given a very characteristic flavor to the food — rather like soy sauce in Japanese and Chinese cookery today.

SALT BEEF AND PORK

Whereas humbler folk would have to make the meat of their single pig last them during the winter, the feudal nobility must have eaten a good deal of preserved meat, winter and summer. The Middle Ages were a time when warfare was very much concerned with the retention of strongly garrisoned castles. And since a fortress can hold out against an enemy only as long as it has a food supply, a primary concern of a castle's commander (or more likely his wife) was maintaining a good store of food. Now, since the only way of preserving food known to the Middle Ages was by salting or smoking, knights and men-at-arms lived almost entirely on preserved meat. They had to keep eating up their stores before they went bad. Salt beef would not keep forever, and one of the duties of the chatelaine, or lady of the castle, was to make sure that the cooks used the oldest casks of beef first, instead of simply saving themselves trouble by pulling out the ones nearest to the storeroom door.

The difficulty of supplying food to armies in the field was one which medieval generals usually found insurmountable. Thus medieval wars, though frequent, were seldom of long duration and readily interrupted by truce. Even so, medieval armies tended to melt away because of lack of supplies, or lose many more men through dysentery than wounds.

By contrast, Roman commanders had shown great concern for the hygiene and diet of their armies. The legions had been provided for in the field and in winter quarters by an elaborate commissariat system, and on the whole they had been well fed. Medieval armies were often chaotically run. Moreover, the staple ration of the Romans, wheat, could be obtained anywhere and was not difficult to store, so that shortages were temporary. But preserved meat, the medieval standby, could only be got during the autumn slaughter of the herds and might be unobtainable overseas.

When Saint Louis, king of France, invaded Egypt in 1250, he brought with him vast supplies of bacon and pork on which to feed his troops. There was no hope of getting more pork to renew his supplies in Egypt, because there was not a single pig in the country north of Nubia; moreover the preserved sides of bacon which the French carried with them were highly susceptible to fly infestation. Consequently the whole French army suffered dreadfully from dysentery. Finally Louis was forced to surrender. One of the terms in the treaty was that the crusaders would be allowed to keep their supplies of preserved pork. This clause was promptly broken by the Muslim conquerors, who had a religious abhorrence of pork. They set fire to the food supplies of Louis' army. The piles of bacon were so big, says Joinville, one of Louis' companions, that they took three days to burn up.

It is not surprising that Christian armies, eating bacon and drinking wine or beer, were frequently overcome by Muslim ones, who ate much lighter fare — flaps of barley bread, yogurt, dates, rice, and mutton taken fresh from herds of sheep accompanying the armies. No Muslim army was ever so drunk that it could not get into formation or face the enemy, something that frequently happened in the case of Christian armies, who demanded supplies of wine or beer wherever they were.

THE NEED FOR SPICES

The conflict between crusaders and Saracens is a good point to turn back to the vexed question of why medieval cooks used so much spice. The old-fashioned view was that spices were put in to disguise the taste of the inevitable salt in the meat. "At a time when overkept meats and fish were freely used," writes Mead, "spice was employed to cover up the incipient decay." There is a lot to be said for this point of view. But in addition salt meats were often cooked with accompaniments, such as beans and bread crumbs, added to the meat to extract some of the salt from it, and these accompaniments would have tasted insufferably bland unless they had been spiced up.

All this may be true but it does not explain why medieval people also spiced their wines as well. Rarely was any drink, whether wine or mead, served up unmixed. A favorite was hippocras, supposed to have been an invention of Hippocrates. Hippocras was compounded of wine (red or white), ginger, cinnamon, pomegranate, grains, sugar, and sunflower seeds. This was the hippocras prepared for those of high degree — we shall see in a moment that your social standing determined what you were supposed to eat in the Middle Ages. For ordinary folk hippocras would merely be wine flavored with ginger, cinnamon, long pepper, and clarified honey. Was medieval wine all so sour and acid that it needed all these additives to make it potable? It is difficult to believe this. Nor is it easy to see why, just because the beef tasted salty, people should be continually chewing candies (the word comes from Candia in Crete, one of the places whence sugar was imported) highly flavored with spices.

The real reasons why medieval folk liked spices so much seem to have been complex. Spices were associated with the mysterious East and in particular with the prestigious rulers of Egypt and Syria, who had at their command invincible armies, spendid palaces, apparently unlimited wealth, and all the learning, science, and culture that Europe was slowly beginning to absorb through her contacts with Islam in Spain and the Holy Land. And Islamic cookery contained much spices, too. It is easy to see why. In warm climates the process of decay runs with alarming swiftness. Even meat killed the same day has to be smothered in spices before it appears on the table if the flavor of putrefaction is not to spoil the dish. Hence a passion for spicy food may have owed a good deal to admiring imitation.

Spices were also considered to be essential to health. "Whatever medicines are applicable to nature," wrote Roger Bacon (1214– 1294), an English Franciscan, "are fragrant, and with ease and speed refresh the spirits, are true cordials. But spices are such, therefore true cordials." Mead agrees with this view: "Most men knew that the enormous amount of meat served for a feast, or even for an ordinary meal, imposed a heavy burden upon the digestion, and hence they used cinnamon and cardamom and ginger and many other spices to whip up the action of the stomach."

A MEDIEVAL FEAST

A medieval dinner was not merely an occasion when people ate to relieve the pangs of hunger, or partook of spices to keep themselves in good health and secure longevity. It was the centerpoint of medieval culture. A great kitchen, such as the Prior's Kitchen at Durham, which is fortunately still in existence, was a sort of artist's studio, where masterpieces were created in sugar and pastry, delights for the eye as well as for the taste. It is not difficult to imagine the Priory cook devising one of those "subtleties" as they were called in the Middle Ages, for Prior Washington (forebear of George Washington) and working into it with colored sugar and icing the red and white stripes which were a feature of the Washington family coat of arms.

SUBTLETIES

Even the most elaborate wedding cake of modern times pales before the sugar sculptures of the subleties. These cakes, if that is what we should call them, took a hundred different forms: miniature castles and cathedrals, figures of men and women, birds, animals, mythological monsters. Virtually every subtlety would have a motto attached to it. One subtlety, of Saint Edward and Saint Louis in full armor, holding between them the figures of King Henry VI, carried an entire ballad. It was followed by a jelly on which were the words and music of *Te Deum laudamus* ("We praise Thee, God," a medieval hymn of thanksgiving).

At the coronation feast of Henry V there was a subtlety of a swan sitting on a green stock, six cygnets, and twenty-four other swans. They bore mottoes such as "Look at the king and you will see righteousness," and "Noble honor and joy,' in their beaks. The subtleties of the second course were antelopes, and those of the third eagles covered with gold.

Not just the subtleties but every dish at great feasts could be gilded, colored with saffron and other herbs, sculpted, and adorned. At the coronation banquet of Henry V the king was served frumenty with venison, "Viand royal" (beef à la king) planted with lozenges of gold, a boar's head in a gilded castle, with his tusks added. There followed beef boiled with mutton, stewed capon, roasted cygnet, roasted heron, a great pike, a dish of sliced meat carved into the shape of lions, a royal custard with a gold leopard sitting on it and holding a *fleur-de-lis*, a fritter made to look like a sun, with a *fleur-de-lis* on it. All these lions and *fleurs-de-lis* were emblematic of the fact that young Henry had just married the daughter of the French king.

It was small wonder that cooks who could create such culinary masterpieces, delights to the eye and the mind as well as to the taste, should have been greatly honored in the Middle Ages. On state occasions the cook joined the procession into the Great Hall where the meals were to be eaten. He had the honor of carrying the first dish to the table. He enjoyed the coziest seat in the kitchen, by the chimney corner, and as a mark of rank he carried a great wooden spoon. This was used for tasting the soup, and also for chastising his assistants.

There could be no doubt that the art of dining reached its height during the Middle Ages. Meals took place in a gorgeous setting, in some great hall with a hammer-beam roof. While the banquet progressed, musicians played their instruments from the minstrels' gallery at the end of the hall and poets sang their verses before the assembled company. The liveries of the retainers and the gorgeous dress of the company vied with the bright-hued tapestries which hung the walls to catch the eye.

Dogs accompanied their masters and mistresses to dinner, and sat under the table amidst the rushes with which the floor was strewn, munching the bones and doubtless begging for tidbits.

There is no question but that amidst all this grandeur, a great deal of solid eating was done. At the installation of Archbiship Neville at York in 1467 a partial list of the food consumed included 300 quarters of wheat, 300 tuns of ale, 100 tuns of wine, 1 pipe of hippocras, 104 oxen, 6 wild bulls, 1,000 sheep, 304 calves, 304 suckling pigs, 400 swans, 2,000 geese, 1,000 capons, 2,000 pigs, 104 peacocks, 13,500 birds of all kinds, and 500 or more stags, bucks and roes. There were 1,500 hot vension pasties, 608 pikes and breams, 12 porpoises and seals, 13,000 dishes of jelly, cold baked tarts, hot and cold custards, and "spices, sugared delicacies and wafers aplenty."

There were six thousand guests at this dinner, but even so the amount of food and wine gives an enormous allowance for each person. No wonder that England was known as "merry England" in the Middle Ages.

HOSPITALITY

It was not just archbishops who gave splendid feasts. Everybody in the Middle Ages entertained friends and neighbors to the best of their ability — or even beyond it. One of the characters in the "Prologue" to *The Canterbury Tales* is a franklin, or landowner. Geoffrey Chaucer (1340– 1400) tells of a pilgrimage to the shrine of Saint Thomas at Canterbury, a journey during which each of the principal characters tells a story. Though the stories are imaginary the people mentioned in it may have been real — or drawn from real-life observation.

Real or imaginary, Chaucer's franklin was the ideal kind of neighbor to have. He was looked on as a veritable Saint Julian, the patron saint of hospitality, by everybody in this part of the country. "It snowed in his house of food and drink," says Chaucer expressively. Whereas most medieval people put up their dining tables once, or at the most twice, a day, the franklin had his standing all the time, ready laid for whoever might drop in and feel disposed to eat.

Of course the franklin himself liked to eat, as well as dispense hospitality. He started the day with a piece of bread in a glass of wine. The bread was usually toasted, hence the expression "a toast," meaning drinking someone's health. At subsequent meals he would sample his own bread and ale, made on the premises, his roast meat, of which he was very fond, his partridges — he raised his own — his fish, such as bream or luce, of which he had fish ponds full, or whatever might be the delicacy of the season.

Hospitality to strangers was considered a great virtue. But more than that, it was a political and social asset of the highest quality. Chaucer's franklin, although he probably kept open house because he was a jolly fellow and loved company, certainly reaped the rewards of his kindness to his friends and neighbors. When the court of the Justices of the King's Peace met, there was the franklin, sitting in the middle of the bench of judges, presiding over them. He was so popular that he was elected again and again as a Member of Parliament, a "Knight of the Shire" by his neighbors. There he would have a difficult and arduous task in persuading the King not to ask for too heavy taxes, but he would also be in a good position to gain the ear of important people in court and try to influence them to do what he wanted in the interest of local politics.

POLITICS AND ENTERTAINING

In fact, a man's standing during the Middle Ages was intimately tied up with how many dinners he gave and how good his cook was. Really important people, such as the great feudal nobles, kept open house. Everybody who dropped in to dinner with them would be served according to his degree, but nobody would go away unsatisfied. On departure guests would bless the hospitable heart of their host and offer to serve him — if only with their prayers.

Most nobles, such as that great warlord of fifteenth-century England, the Earl of Warwick, expected substantial services from the thousands they fed at their table every day. Eveyone could take his turn at the table and carry away as much meat as he could skewer on a dagger, as well as broth, ale, and bread. The more able-bodied of Warwick's guests would be drawn toward becoming his permanent retainers, servants or soldiers wearing his livery and badge — the Bear with Ragged Staff — and would fight for him if need be. Quarrels among these private armies led to many of the bickerings that characterized the Middle Ages, but no one wished to be the first to give them up. Finally the Wars of the Roses in the fifteenth century killed off so many noblemen that it was relatively easy for Henry VII, who emerged as victor in the long conflict, to ban them.

In spite of this prohibition, most noblemen felt that it was inconsistent with their dignity not to have a great household of retainers. As late as 1561, the Earl of Derby had 140 servants and "the ordinary weekly consumption of the household was about one ox, a dozen calves, a score of sheep, fifteen hogsheads of ale, and plenty of bread, fish, and poultry."

MONASTERIES

One reason hospitality was regarded as such a great virtue was that, unless you could claim someone's shelter, you might well go without supper or a bed, especially if you were traveling. There were inns, such as the Tabard in Southwark, London, where the Canterbury pilgrims started their journey, but these were few and far between. Many districts in England boasted no inns, at all and there were whole countries, like Ireland and Scotland, which were in the same fix. In places such as these, the benighted traveler would drop in at some manor house, such as the franklin's, and ask for a meal and shelter for the night. If he were lucky, he would find a host who had a good cook, like the franklin's, whose sauces always had to be sharp and piquant to please his master.

But better even than a manor house for the weary traveler was the sound of a cloister bell ringing the Angelus. Monks and nuns were always hospitable, and although they ate a special diet themselves, they would serve a hungry traveler ordinary fare.

In addition to fasting for thirty-six days in Lent, like the whole of Christendom, the religious observed meatless days (called days of abstinence) when they lived on vegetables, fish, and eggs. In the stricter orders monks and nuns might well fast for the greater part of the year. Meat would only appear on the table at a great feast of the church, or be served to the sick in the infirmary. Convent and monastery fare was modeled on the diet of the poor — vegetables, bread, dairy products, with beer to drink. Monks of the Cistercian Order even carried poverty so far as to eat leftovers. Generally speaking medieval folk do not seem to have relished these. They gave away the remains of their meals to the poor, or to the dogs, including the "trenchers" — flat plates made from bread — on which they had eaten the meal.

In Cistercian abbeys there was often only one meal. "If they eat supper, the remains of their lunch are dished up again, with the difference that, instead of the two cooked dishes, fresh vegetables, if they are to be had, are served."

An austere vegetable diet was supposed to subdue the lusts of the flesh. It probably kept the monks and nuns much healthier than the heavy diet of meat favored by laymen and laywomen.

During the Middle Ages, monasteries and nunneries became the refuge of people with good table manners. One of the characters in the *Canterbury Tales* is the ladylike prioress, Madame Eglentyne.

She had been well taught etiquette, and when she ate, crumbs did not fall from her mouth. She did not push her fingers deep into the sauce, and when she picked something up from the dish, she took care that nothing dripped onto her dress. She always wanted to behave in as polite a way as possible. So she wiped her upper lip thoroughly so that spots of grease did not appear on the surface of her drink once she had sipped it. She reached for what she wanted from the table in a very restrained way, and truly she was very good humoured and had a pleasant and amiable manner. She liked to behave as they do at court, in a stately and dignified way, and thus to be held worthy to be given reverence.

The desire to be respected by their company because they knew how to behave at table was very widespread among the English upper classes at this time. Girls of good family were sent to nunneries, such as that run by Madame Eglentyne at Bow in London, to learn the social graces. Boys were sent away from home to live with relatives and friends and to learn everything connected with the courtesy which the Middle Ages had so much at heart. No well-educated young man, such as the squire in the *Canterbury Tales*, would think of sitting down to table until he had served his father and carved for him.

> Courteous he was, lowly and servicable
> And carved before his father at the table.

GLUTTONY

The monastic dislike of overeating or overdrinking had as its general counterpart the discountenancing of gluttony in society as a whole. Gluttony was one of the seven deadly sins of the Middle Ages, the others being Pride, Wrath, Envy, Lust, Avarice, and Sloth. Though it has never been officially demoted from being a sin by the church, you can go a long way nowadays without hearing a single sermon on it. (Or if you do, it is called intemperence and denounces overdrinking rather than overeating.) Some countries took gluttony much more seriously than others. In Scotland it became not merely a sin but a crime. Scots found guilty of overeating were strangled with a withy, or peeled willow wand (rope was scarce in Scotland), or drowned in a running stream. Severe ''sumptuary laws'' telling the poor what they must eat and what they might not were also issued.

This attitude must have issued from the natural Puritanism of the Scots, because food was not scarce in Lowland Scotland. Immense herds of cattle were raised, and many of them were butchered on the spot, for the sake of their tallow and hides, thus providing plenty of meat. Everybody ate oatmeal as porridge or bannocks, and thrived on it. Scots raiders were formidable because of the mobility afforded to them by their staple food. They could strike across the English border, carrying all the supplies they needed — a bag of oatmeal and an iron griddle — on the crupper of their swift Galloway nags. Fish also swarmed in Scotlands lakes and rivers. Apprentices in their articles stipulated that they should not be required to eat smoked salmon more than twice a week.

SUMPTUARY LAWS

"Tell me what you eat," said the great French writer on gastronomy, Anthelme Brillat-Savarin (1755 – 1826), "and I will tell you what you are." This dictum was certainly true of the Middle Ages. Officially speaking, a Roman Emperor had been merely an ordinary Roman citizen, carrying out a particular job. He would never have dared to suggest that certain kinds of food should be reserved for his consumption alone. But medieval kings did this repeatedly. An Act of Parliament of 1320 declared all whales, dolphins, porpoises, and sturgeon "Fishes Royal." As such they must be offered for the royal table or allowed to swim free in the seas.*

The royal fondness for cetacean meat is merely one example of how tastes in food change over the centuries. I ate whale meat once during World War II and have no desire ever to taste it again. In the Middle Ages, however, it was apparently considered delicious, as were such other strange-sounding dishes as cormorant, swan, peacock, and seal. The peacock symbolized the "eyes of the world" turned on the knight and was often served gilded with tail feathers — the "eyes" — intact. Many of these dishes would be extremely unappetizing to modern tastes. Mead tells us, for example, that "the flesh of the whale itself remains hard and indigestible even after 24 hours of cooking."

Swans are no longer eaten in England, but they are still regarded as royal — or at least special — birds. Every year, in a ceremony called swan upping, the birds are rounded up and nicked in a particular way to show that they belong either to the Queen or to the Livery Companies of the City of London. This has the effect of making all swans private property and a protected species.

At medieval feasts a great distinction was made between high and low social groups by having the high group sit at high table, a table placed at the head of the hall and standing crosswise to the others. This was often a

---

*This royal prerogative still exists and was recently invoked by the Queen's agents — in this instance the British Museum, Natural History — to compel a private zoo to release a porpoise called Popsie, which had been washed up on the shore and nursed back to health by the zoo staff.

"table dormant," a piece of regular furniture with fixed legs, in contrast to the trestle table used by the commons, which were dismantled at the end of the meal. The distinction between high table and low is still observed in most colleges at the ancient English universities, and the tradition that the food served at high table differs (for the better) from that served at low is still firmly believed by most undergraduates.

If you were not grand enough to have separate tables but sat at one with your household, the distinction between the different degrees was marked by the position of the salt cellar. This cellar, a tall, handsome piece of silver plate, stood in the middle of the table. Those of high degree sat "above the salt" while lesser mortals sat below.

VENISON

There was one of the "royal foods" in particular which English sovereigns tried to appropriate to themselves, and this was venison. Venison was much more relished in the Middle Ages than it is now, because it was impossible to obtain a good steak then. The cattle were small, spindly, tough, and lean, whereas venision from the red, roe, or fallow deer which browsed in the great forests, was juicy and well flavored. "How fat he is!" exclaimed King John as he saw a buck being cut up, and then he added in the irreverent way which made him so obnoxious to religious folk, "And yet the rascal never heard Mass!"

The desire for venison, whether as a roast haunch, a numbles pie, or venison collops, had to be curbed by ordinary folk, because all venison belonged to the king, and those who ate it courted the most extreme penalties.

Enormous royal forests covered virtually the whole country. Nobody could hunt there except for the King and a few chosen favorites, such as bishops and abbots on their way to the royal council. Even to hunt a deer *outside* a royal forest was extremely risky, because it might be one which the King had chased but which had escaped him. To walk a greyhound through a forest, even to wear Lincoln green (the color of foresters' official garb) unauthorized would bring you within reach of the Forest Laws. The penalties for deer poaching varied from reign to reign. At the acme of their severity they might entail blinding and castration.

REACTION TO THE FOREST LAWS

The reaction to the declaration of a royal monopoly of venison by the medieval English kings took two forms. One was that of the outlaws, such as that hero of English folklore, Robin Hood, who was usually to be found "in the parks, killing the King's deer." There is some suggestion that in real life Robin Hood may have been a follower of Simon de Montfort, a nobleman who led the thirteenth-century Barons' War against the misrule of Henry III. The other form of reaction to the Forest Laws was out-and-out rebellion. The grievances of the English against the Forest Laws and other aspects of royal tyranny resulted in their forcing their kings to make them grants of liberities by charter, such as Magna Carta, 1215, and Parlimentary representation. In time the original harsh forest jurisdication was watered down. Subjects were even allowed to own their own deer parks and hunt their own deer if they wanted to.

DEER PARKS AND OAK TREES

There were other effects of the craze for venison. If you owned a deer park, you had to fence it to keep the deer in and the poachers out. The wood preferred for paling deer parks was oak, and eventually more oak trees grew in England than anywhere else in the world — specially planted to provide the fencing for deer parks. By the sixteenth century, many of the landed gentry had become impoverished by economic changes and were ready to sell their standing oak trees, thus many of them became available for shipbuilding.

A difficult, awkward wood to work with, oak has one interesting quality, which the shipbuilders were soon to discover. A cannon ball fired into an oak beam does not drive it into splinters. The tough fibers of the oak compress the ball so that it simply embeds itself in the wood. In any battle between wooden ships, the casualties from splinters were greater than those from enemy shot, so by and large those who sailed in an oak-built ship would always suffer less than those sailing in a ship built from some other wood.

5.

The Search For Spices

FLOW OF SPICES RESTRICTED

On the whole, medieval people were hard-headed and practical. The English King who put an end to the Wars of the Roses, Henry VII, was a good example. He corrected the royal accounts with his own hand, and he was fond of indulging in private speculation, such as sending cargoes of his own abroad. Henry was shrewd, businesss-like, and prudent — too prudent, as it turned out. With his usual caution, he turned down what afterward proved to the be the most successful investment ever undertaken. It was a suggestion by a Genoese sailor named Christopher Columbus that the King should finance a voyage of exploration to sail directly to the countries where the spices grew — India, Japan, and China. Such a trade route, if established, would bypass the stranglehold over the existing traffic in spices.

During the fifteenth century the Sarocen dynasties of the Near East, against whom Saint Louis had fought, had been overthrown by a new and extremely fanatical group of rulers, the Ottoman Turks.

The Turks wanted to hit at Christendom in whatever way they could. One obvious way was to ask them much more for the spices that flowed from the Far East, through the Near East, into Europe — 2,500 tons a year through Venice alone. So the Turks raised the export taxes on spices to such a height that by the time a cargo of spices left Aleppo, in the eastern Mediterranean, it cost 800 percent more than it had when it left India.

Through the price of spices had gone up, the demand for them had increased. When Gluttony was on his way to church to hear Mass, make his confession, and then sin no more, says a late medieval poem, he passed the house of Betty the alewife, who bade him good morrow. "I have good ale, Gluttony," she said, "would you like to try it?"

Gluttony's reply was, "Have you any hot spices?" When Betty reeled off the list, pepper and peony seed, fennel seed and garlic, Gluttony decided he would go in and try the ale.

In England, and in Europe as a whole, the common folk could afford to spend more on food then formerly, because they were receiving much better wages for their work in the fields. The Black Death had diminished the number of laborers so much that landowners often had to compete for their services. Much of the money they got went in food. The author of the poem just quoted is horrified that English laborers should now be asking for new kinds of food in alehouses — the kinds formerly eaten only by the rich.

One of the new kinds of food that were becoming popular as the Middle Ages drew to an end was the stockfish, or dried cod. Cod, or "John Dory," was plentiful because the fishing fleets were now sailing farther afield. Their range was extended even more widely when an explorer whom Henry VII did decide to finance, John Cabot, discovered North America. In 1497 Cabot made a landfall at Cape Breton Island (Nova Scotia) and then sailed along the southern shores of Newfoundland, where he noted the abundance of codfish on the Grand Banks. The European fishing fleets, which had hitherto operated off Norway or Iceland, now migrated to Newfoundland for the summer. The fish were caught, gutted, and hung on wooden "stocks" or frames on the beach to dry. To feed themselves during these summer excursions, fishermen cooked up huge fish stews in a pot called a *chaudière,* hence our word "chowder."

Stockfish was tasteless and so hard that it had to be soaked for at least twenty-four hours to make it palatable. And even then a spiced sauce was needed to disguise the flavor — a *sauce jaune,* made from ginger; *sauce verte,* made from ginger, cloves, and cardamom; or *sauce cameline,* made from cinnamon, ginger, cloves, cardamom, mace, and long pepper. All these ingredients were products of the Far East. Even mustard sauce (mustard itself is a common European field crop) had to be made with turmeric, grown in Asia.

It was very tantalizing that Europeans should want spices so badly and yet have to pay through the nose to the Ottoman middlemen. They knew all about where spices really came from through the writings of a European merchant who had actually traveled to the Far East.

MARCO POLO, SPICE AGENT

Marco Polo had first visited the court of Kublai Khan with his father Marco and Uncle Matteo in 1272. Young Polo had not merely traveled over much of China and Burma, he had returned home via the Spice Islands (Moluccas) themselves, sailing down the South China Sea through the Strait of Malacca, across the Indian Ocean, up the west coast of India to the head of the Persian Gulf. The purpose of the voyage had been to conduct a Molgol princess to her future bridegroom, the Khan of Persia. By the end of the voyage only eighteen of the original voyagers were left, including the Polos, the princess, and one of the Mongol envoys. The others had died, presumably of scurvy, a deficiency disease caused by lack of vitamin C.

When Marco got back to his home town, Venice, in 1295, he was a millionaire. He would probably have spent his life in peaceful retirement and no one would ever have heard of his travels. But in 1298 there was a war between Venice and her great commercial rival, Genoa. Marco was captured at sea while commanding a galley. In prison he whiled away the monotony of captivity by dictating his travels to a fellow prisoner, and it was later transcribed and widely read. It became one of the most influential books ever written.

Marco Polo's fellow Venetians were more than a little skeptical of his accounts of the riches of the East. They nicknamed him "Marco Millions." Not all Italians laughed at his book, however. One of them read about China, with its "great abundance of ginger, galingale, spikenard, and many other kinds of spices. Canton is the harbour where all the ships of India came, with much costly merchandise. . . . I assure you that for one shipload of pepper that goes to Alexandria or elsewhere to be taken to Christian lands, there comes an hundred to the port of Canton.'' This same reader — his name was Christopher Columbus, and he has left his name on the flyleaf of the book, now preserved in Seville — read everything that Marco Polo had to say and pondered on it until it became an obsession. He dreamed of discovering a way to Cypangu (Japan) with its palaces roofed in gold.

BARRIERS TO THE SPICE ISLANDS

Other readers also put Polo's book to good profit. One of the Catalan cartographers of Barcelona drew up a map based on the Venetian's travels, the Catalan Map of 1375. On this map could be seen Europe, on the one hand, and on the other "the sea of the Indian Islands, in which grow the spices." Between Europe and the Spice Islands there were two great barriers, one political, the other geographical. The political one was the Ottoman Empire. The Ottomans would never be prepared to let anyone travel through their domains to look for spices. So there was no possibility of making the journey that the Polos had made earlier. The other barrier was a geographical one, the continent of Africa. Nobody knew how far south it stretched, because no one had ever circumnavigated it — or not in recent times.

The most eminent geographers of the day were the Arabs. But they had little desire to escape from the Ptolemaic conception of the world as it was known to the ancient Greeks, and they were not prepared to speculate about possible routes to unknown continents. Moreover, they had a horror of the western ocean beyond the European and African continents, which they referred to as "the Green Sea of Darkness." Nobody should be so foolish as to venture over this sea to discover its limits. If he tried it, he might meet the fate that, according to legend, met those who actually sailed to the Equator — they were engulfed by the torrid waters of the ocean, which there reached boiling point. Or if he escaped boiling alive, he would simply sail off the edge of the world.

The man who was to have the courage to prove all the geographers in the world wrong and point out the way to the spices of the East did so through his connection with quite another condiment — salt.

HENRY THE NAVIGATOR

Henry the Navigator (1394 – 1460) was the fourth son of King John I of Portugal and English Queen, Philippa of Lancaster. As a member of a crusading expedition sent to Ceuta, in North Africa in 1415, he had learned from the Arab prisoners he interrogated of the extent of the great trans-Saharan salt trade. Salt was a commodity that nobody could do without, however primitive or undeveloped they might be. So caravans of salt traders started from the Mediterranean coast, where salt was dried out in salt pans, crossed the Sahara along well-frequented routes,* moving from one oasis to another, and penetrated into the great forests south of the desert. From there the Arab caravans returned with gold dust, ivory, goat skins of the famous ''Morocco'' leather (which was merely sold, not tanned, in Morocco), and slaves.

The information provided by the prisoners of Ceuta enabled Henry to build up a mental map of the great continent. If plodding camels could penetrate into its utmost recesses, then it ought not to be too big for a Portuguese caravel to circumnavigate.

The caravel was a light handy craft evolved by the Portuguese navigators, and it owed a lot to the lines of the Arab dhows. With singleminded purpose Henry now retired from the court at Lisbon to the windswept promontory of Cape St. Vincent, in the extreme south of Portugal. There he set up a school for explorers at a place called Sagres and surrounded himself with the best Jewish and Arab cartographers of the day.

When he consulted them about the feasibility of a voyage around Africa, they were unanimous in giving a discouraging reply. Even if an exploring caravel managed to round Cape Bojador, the ''bulging cape'' which thrust out into the Atlantic from the African continent, it could never make the return trip to Portugal, because the prevailing northeast wind would drive it down the coast. Moreover, sandbanks along the coast would soon force the Portuguese sailors off shore and out to sea, beyond the known landmarks, whence they could never recover their positon.

Henry listened respectfully to the learned men of his entourage, then issued his orders to the captains he sent southward. These orders were always the same: ''Go as far as you can.''

Curiously enough spices played only a part in the great navigator's desire to round Africa. He principally wanted to inflict a decisive defeat on the Muslims, from whom Portugal had only recently freed itself (they still held part of Spain), and he believed he might be able to a make contact with a legendary Christian king, named Prester John, who was supposed to be living somewhere in Africa.

---

*There were several of these routes: from Morocco to Cairo by In Salah and Ghudamis (in modern Algeria); from Lake Chad to Marzuq and Tripoli (in modern Libya); from Kano (Nigeria) and Zinder (Niger) to Tripoli by Aïr (Niger) and Ghiat (Libya); from Timbuktu (Neali) to Morocco.

START OF THE SLAVE TRADE

Henry's persistence wore down skeptical captains, mutinous crews, and even the navigational difficulties of the African coast. In 1434 Gil Eannes rounded Cape Bojador, proving that it could be done. In 1441 Gonçalves captured some Africans and brought them back to Portugal, where they could be instructed in Christianity and trained as interpreters. Slave trading had not been one of Henry's original objectives, but it made the business of exploration much more attractive to other Portuguese, as did the discovery of gold at Rio de Oro in 1443.

Just before he died, in 1459, Henry saw the results of the forty years of exploration he had directed summarized by an Italian. Fra Mauro, a cartographer, drew up a Map of the World showing 2,000 miles of coastline which explor Henry's explorers had charted.

There was no stopping the Portuguese explorers now, because pepper had been discovered growing on the African coast. Who knew what other spices might be waiting to be discovered there? In 1488 Batholomew Dias was blown around the southern headland of the African coast. He named the southernmost point Cape of Storms, but when he got home, King John II promptly changed the name to Cape of Good Hope. "This discovery," he told Dias, "gives us a good hope of reaching India."

DA GAMA

The aspirations of a century were at last realized when an expedition led by Vasco da Gama cast anchor in the port of Calicut on the west coast of India on May 20, 1498. It was the first time that a European ship had entered Indian waters since the "well-built craft of the Javannah," (Roman ships) had made their last voyage from Roman Egypt.

The Arab merchants in Calicut were unable to contain their fury at the sight of the European interlopers. "The devil take you!" exclaimed one of them as he met a Portuguese officer in the port. "What are you doing here?" "We have come in search of spices and Christians," replied the Portuguese.

The Indian King of Calicut was a little friendlier. He refused to sign a treaty with the King of Portugal, but he did agree to allow da Gama to take away a small cargo of spices — in exchange for gold and silver. More than a thousand years had passed since the last Roman ship left India, but the Indians had not changed. The Portugese, who had expected to barter with glass beads, hawks' bells, and woolen cloth, were speechless.

Da Gama's chagrin at having to pay cash for his spices was mitigated by the price he got for them after his 24,000-mile return trip to Lisbon had ended. A third of the original ship's crew had died, no doubt from scurvy, but that simply meant there were fewer to share in the profits.

COLUMBUS

One of the reasons why da Gama had been so keen to sail was that he had heard a report (which he did not believe) that Christopher Columbus had discovered a sea route to the Indies by sailing *westward*. At least it was the belief of the great Genoese navigator that he had reached the Indies. To the end of his life he maintained that his four voyages (1492 – 1503) had resulted not in the discovery of new lands (there was no such place as America in Ptolemy's geography) but in that of Cypangu and the mainland of Asia. As "proof" of his discoveries, he produced wild plants which he asserted to be cinnamon, Chinese rhubarb, and coconut (none were). His monomania led him to call the natives of the newly discovered island "Indians," and he strained his ears in the hope of catching a few words of Japanese. One word which he noted down in his journal was to become a permanent addition to the vocabulary of eating — "cannibal." Columbus had not quite caught a name given to him by one of the Indians. It was correctly "Carib." The original inhabitants of the Caribbean were cannibals, but they only ate the enemies they had killed in battle.

THE PORTUGUESE SPICE EMPIRE

The two Iberian powers were now running neck and neck to acquire more and more overseas possessions. In the Indian Ocean proconsuls such as Francisco de Almeida (1505 – 09) and Alfonso de Albuquerque (1509 – 15) had built up a vast Portuguese empire. Their aim was to keep exclusive Portuguese control of the newly discovered sea routes to the East, exploit the spice trade, and eliminate all rivals, whether Arab traders or Spanish interlopers.

The search for spices, which had started as a crusade against Muslim domination, had now turned into a gigantic pirate's raid, which was to make the name "European" stink for centuries. As Almeida himself said, a Chinese junkman knew more about honor and chivalry than any knight in Christendom.

Ironically, it was on the Muslim powers of the Far East that the full weight of Portuguese conquest was to fall — ironically because it was the fault of their coreligionists of the Middle East that the Portuguese were there in the first place. Not only had Turks raised the price of spices, but the Arabs had instilled in Europeans a limitless belief in their medical power.

Thanks to the teachings of Arab medicine, Europeans now believed that spices were a panacea, able to promote longevity and ward off infection. Plague doctors walked through the pest-ridden streets of Europe holding to their noses a "pomander," or dried orange studded with cloves. After a hard day's battle, Charles the Bold of Burgundy would order enough bodies to be cleared from the battlefield to let him sit down and drink a cup of the hot spiced wine as a restorative. Spices could also increase virility — or so it was believed by the Arabs. During his travels in the East in 1500, Ludovico de Varthema, a Portuguese commercial spy, had been told that Arab women gave their lovers pepper, cinnamon, cloves, and spices as an aphrodisiac.

In order to monoplize the Indian Ocean, an Arab preserve, the Portuguese would be obliged to fight every Arab power in the area: the states of the Persian Gulf coast, the rulers of western India, the seafaring Malays, and the sultans of the Spice Islands of Java, Sumatra, and Malacca.

It says a lot for the Portuguese that they even took on this daunting tasks, but, astonishingly, they succeeded at it. In an attempt to checkmate the Portuguese advance, the Ottoman Turks had a special fleet built on the Red Sea, equipped it with monster cannon, and in 1507 sent it into Indian waters. After initial victories, the combined Muslim fleet from Egypt, Calicut, and Gujerat was destroyed by Francisco de Almeida off Diu in 1509. This was to be one of the most decisive battles in history. The Europeans were to remain continually victorious at sea over the fleets of other continents until the battle of Tsuchima, in 1905, when Japan defeated Russia at sea.

At the time, the battle of Diu seemed just another milestone in the grim Portuguese advance. The Portuguese wanted three things: strategically placed fortresses by the sea from which their fleets could control the trade routes, naval bases where they could repair the ravages of the tropics on ships and men, and "factories" or trading posts where they could collect spices from the primary producers.

Soon no trading junk or dhow could put to sea unless it carried a license from the Portuguese viceroy. Portugal, which, it must be remembered, was only a tiny nation with less than a million inhabitants, controlled the cloves from Amboyna in the Moluccas, the nutmegs from Banda and the Celebes, the cinnamon from Ceylon, the pepper from the Malabar coast, and the ginger of China.

MAGELLAN

The first real challenge to the Portuguese monopoly in the Indian Ocean came, surprisingly enough, from a Portuguese. Ferdinand Magellan had served in India under Almeida in 1504. Between 1504 and 1511 he had been stationed on the Spice Islands. Behind him, westward, lay the route he had come by, a long chain of Portuguese staging posts between Lisbon and Ternate, the farthest possession in the Spice Islands. Eastward, what might there not be? Perhaps, Magellan thought, there might be a new sea route which would run from the islands, circling America and heading eastward to Spain.

Within a short time Magellan had shifted his allegiance from Portugal to Spain. Though it had taken Columbus eight years to persuade Ferdinand and Isabella to give him an expedition to sail to Cypangu, it took only a year for Magellan to persuade Charles V of Spain to give him five ships and two years' provisions. The Portuguese renegade had a particularly telling argument. In 1494 the Spanish and Portuguese had tried to sort out their imperial rivalries by signing a treaty, the Tordesillas Agreement. This drew a line across the globe, on the longtitude of 47 degrees west. On one side of this demarcation line any new countries discovered should become Spanish possessions, on the other they were to become Portuguese. The Moluccas, Magellan told Charles, an important group of the Spice Islands, lay on the Spanish side of the demarcation line, but there was no means of establishing possession of the Moluccas unless an expedition could be sent there. It would be ensuring disaster to take the conventional route, past so many strong Portuguese fortresses and naval bases, so the flotilla must sail westward, around America.

Magellan does not seem to have raised the point with Charles that perhaps the American continent continued southward until it merged with the great southern continent that many geographers believed covered the South Pole. No doubt, though, this idea occupied his mind as he began to sail south along the Brazilian coast in 1509, farther south than anyone had ever sailed before.

He was now faced with one of the most difficult feats of navigation that could present itself to any captain — threading the narrow straits that now bears his name. There were several mutinies, but Magellan suppressed them.

In a nightmare voyage the circumnavigators headed westward across the Pacific, drinking foul water and eating sawdust and the leather coverings of the masts and yards. The Patagonian giants, whom Magellan had captured and intended to bring home as curiosities, died of scurvy and starvation.

After sighting only two uninhabited islands in the Pacific, Magellan made a landfall in the Ladrones in 1521. A few weeks later he was in the Spice Islands proper, trying to collect a cargo of spices quickly before the Portuguese should find out about the expedition and crush it with overwhelming force.

Halfway through his great adventure, Magellan was killed while helping a native ruler in a local war on Mactan in 1521. It was left to navigator Sebastian del Cano, a Basque who had been one of the mutineers, to bring back the expedition's flagship, *Victoria,* with a cargo of cloves from Tidore.

The voyage of Magellan did not result in a great Spanish spice empire in the Indian Ocean. Charles V sold the Moluccas to Portugal, but retained the Philippines. Charles already had his hands full with empires.

HOLLAND AND ENGLAND ENTER THE BATTLE FOR SPICES

Hitherto the Battle for Spices had been a sort of stately *pavane*, with the Spaniards moving to the west and the Portuguese to the east. Now it suddenly turned into a square dance, as two more partners appeared on the floor, England and Holland.

The English involvement had come about in part because of a quarrel over slave trading. Unwilling to till the fields themselves, the Spanish colonists had at first forced the Indians to work for them. As the harsh treatment to which they were subjected soon exterminated many of the Indian tribes, the Spaniards now had recourse to African slaves. In Brazil, the Portuguese were able to import slaves directly from their African colonies. The Spaniards, who did not possess any colonies in

Africa because of the Treaty of Tordesillas, had to rely on inter-mediaries. Officially, trading with non-Spaniards was forbidden, but in practice the colonists were so short of labor they were quite prepared to buy slaves from anyone.

DRAKE

In an attempt to enforce official policy, the Viceroy of Mexico treacherously attacked English slave trader John Hawkins in the harbor of San Juan de Ulloa. Hawkins had been guaranteed a safe conduct the day before, so his feelings when he managed to fight his way out of San Juan with a few companions may well be imagined. One of these companions was Francis Drake. The Viceroy's action had turned them from more or less peaceful slave traders and adventurers into pirates, and they both became thorns in the flesh to the Spanish in North and South America.

In 1577, el Draco (the Dragon), as the Spaniards called him, demon-strated that Spanish control of the Pacific was not unbreakable. He sailed through the Strait of Magellan, swept up the Peruvian coast, and cap-tured a treasure galleon called the *Fireater*. "We found in her," writes Drake's chaplain, Francis Fletcher, "a certain quantity of jewels and precious stones, 13 chests of rials of plate, 80 pound weight in gold, 26 tons of uncoined silver, two very fair gilt silver drinking bowls, and the like trifles, valued in all at about 360,000 pesos." Drake went on to plunder Valparaiso and Callao, and then to search for the Northwest Passage, which many navigators believed must exist at the northern end of the American continent, just as the Strait of Magellan existed at the southern end. Returning south once more, Drake made contact with the Indians of California, which he claimed for Queen Elizabeth.

Having broken the Spanish monopoly of the Indies, Drake next sailed on into another cherished monopoly, the Portuguese Indian Ocean empire. The Sultan of Ternate, in the Moluccas, was at war with the Portuguese, so he welcomed Drake, sold him several tons of cloves, and said he would be prepared to receive other English traders.

Drake received a warm welcome from Queen Elizabeth when he returned home. She knighted him on the deck of his flagship, the *Golden Hind*, and was gracious enough to accept a share of the treasure he had brought home. It was so enormous that, if if had been put out at compound interest, it would easily pay off Britain's national debt today.

The war, which had begun as a personal feud between Drake and the

King of Spain, now blossomed into a national conflict, as Spain officially declared war on England in 1588. Long before this, enterprising Elizabethans had suggested that a North American colony would make it possible to drive home attacks on the Spanish Main from a base much nearer to the area of conflict than England. Colonies would also produce those spices which had to be bought from abroad. After unsuccessful attempts in Newfoundland and North Carolina, the first permanent English colony was planted in Virginia in 1607.

Holland's involvement in the Spice Wars had begun somewhat differently from England's. The Dutch had started the sixteenth century as subjects of the Holy Roman Empire whose ruler, Charles V, was also king of Spain. Under the rule of his successor, Philip II, they had revolted against high taxation, Spanish mismanagement, and in particular against the Spanish Inquisition. In 1580 Philip had annexed Portugal and in an attempt to hurt the Spanish/Portuguese empire in its most vulnerable place, the Dutch, while still battling with the Spaniards on land, began a great maritime attack on the Portuguese possessions in Africa, Brazil, and in particular the Spice Islands.

In 1602 they defeated a large Portuguese fleet off Bantam, in Java, and took over the island. The inhabitants of Amboyna, Ternate, and Banda welcomed the newcomers. The Portuguese were widely disliked by their subject people because of their religious intolerance. Though it was declared Portuguese policy to mix and mingle with the local people, there was to be no mixture of the Portuguese and local religions.

Everything that was not Roman Catholic was frowned on by the Portuguese conquerors. Everywhere they went, they looted and destroyed temples and mosques, while in Ceylon they disposed of the holiest of all Buddhist relics — the tooth of Buddha — by pounding it into dust and then throwing it in the sea. The dreaded Portuguese Inquisition was at hand to deal with any suspects. A Goanese girl who became a convert to Christianity and married a Portuguese, and who was then reported to have shown signs of a relapse into Hinduism (by wearing a Hindu marriage ornament, for example) would be burned alive in the main square of Goa in an *auto-da-fé*. Her husband would have to stand there, holding a candle, just to prove that he was a good Catholic.

"JOHN COMPANY"

The Dutch celebrated their victory at Bantam by forming a new kind of trading organization — the Dutch East India Company, or *Jan Cam-*

pagnie as it was usually called. This nickname can be translated as "John Company."

The lifeblood of the Dutch East India Company was the capital or stock, which remained permanently invested in the joint stock company. All the stockholders who subscribed this money got a share of the profits at the end of each year. So the Company was wealthier than any individual monarch in Europe, because it could draw on the savings of everyone in Holland. With a gigantic capital of 6½ million guilders, the Company could build fleets, cast its own cannon, hire mercenaries, and construct fortresses, and its charter allowed it to do all these things.

An eminent governor of the Company, Jan Peiterzoon Coen (1587 – 1630) hit on a new overseas policy that would make the Company even richer. Instead of shipping goods from Holland to exchange for spices in Asia, the Dutch simply used their fleets to control all the trade of the Indian Ocean and China seas. With the money obtained from charging tolls from Chinese, Arab, and Malay traders, they bought up all the spices they needed and sent them to Europe, where they were resold at a profit.

The Company would also take drastic measures to deal with competitors in the spice trade. For example, they would sterilize nutmegs by packing them in quicksilver before they were sent abroad. This meant that no one could use these nutmegs to plant new nutmeg trees. Spice-growing islands would curb production in response to Dutch demands; if they did not, all their spice orchards would be rooted up, and the trees thrown into the sea.

One of the interlopers with whom Coen had to deal was a rival company, the English East India Company. In 1599 the Dutch had raised the price of pepper on the London market by 60 percent. English merchants promptly decided that it was hopeless to do business with producers who knew no moderation when it came to price increases. They would start their own company and move into the Indies themselves. The eighty merchants who had founded the Company chose the Indian mainland as a base of operations. In two successive battles at Swally Roads, off Surat, the Company's ships defeated Portuguese fleets sent from Goa to dislodge them. The merchants set up "factories" or trading posts at Masulipatam, Madras, and other ports. The Company even succeeded in setting up a small factory at Cambello, on the island of Amboyna, one of the main spice producers.

But in 1623 John Company reacted. The governor of the East India Company, Jan Coen, arrested the whole English community at Cambello on Amboyna, charged them with all sorts of crimes, and had them executed after fearful tortures. War ought to have broken out, but it did not. In place of the resolute Elizabeth I, the timorous James I now occupied the throne of England. James suffered from a deficiency disease called rickets, which was once very common in Britain. He had been so debilitated by this disease that he had to be helped to walk. Rather than declare war on Holland, he merely protested at the massacre. It was left for Cromwell thirty years later to extract an enormous indemnity from Holland, to be divided amongst the victims' descendants. By that time the English East India Company's interests had been permanently divided to mainland India.

The Dutch, who were highly secretive about the exact location of the various Spice Islands, kept their monopoly until 1788. In that year the brig *Cadet*, out of Salem, Massachusetts, came snooping around the islands of the Dutch East Indies. Salem had a shallow harbor, and her vessels were correspondingly small. As such they could go where many of the large China-tradeships of Europeans could not. Captain Carnes of the *Cadet* found the pepper islands and came home laden not only with pepper but cassia, cinnamon, camphor, and gold dust. The Dutch monopoly was broken, and spices for the first time in history became an ordinary item in the carrying trade.

6.

Food At Sea

The voyages and discoveries which had marked the Spices Revolution had succeeded not because of but in spite of the victualing of the crews and explorers who had carried them out. During the whole of this period, it was felt that one could only keep up one's strength by continually eating and drinking a great deal, and of course what was eaten and drunk must be the same as in Europe. The kinds of food consumed by crews and garrisons in hot climates appears to us, endowed with the benefits of hindsight, the most unsuitable kind of provender that could have been devised.

Thus all provisions of meat were salted. Salted meat does not keep well in a hot climate, and unless specially treated to get the salt out, it is extremely thirst-provoking. Yet as early as the days of Cromwell, it was laid down that sailors in the British navy were to receive two pounds of salt meat or pork a day, or one and a half pounds of fish instead. The meat was usually tainted, if not downright rotten, and even if it were not, all the vitamins that exist in fresh meat had been destroyed by the method of preservation.

Next to meat, the principal part of the ration was bread, usually ship's

92

biscuit. The biscuit (the word comes from *bis* and *cuire* in French, meaning "bake twice") was not baked aboard ship but in port. Sometimes it had been baked the previous year, or the year before that. If it were government issue, it might have been baked as long ago as fifty years.

Making ship's biscuit was an elaborate process which required special categories of workers known as burners, mates, drivers, breakmen and idlemen.

First came the driver; the proper proportions of flour and water being put into a trough, he with his naked and lusty arms beat and thumped and routed and turned the materials until they assumed the state of dough . . . . Then came the breakman. The dough was placed upon a platform, a roller called a break staff, hinged at one end, was placed upon it, and the breakman, riding in side saddle on the other end of the roller, jumped it about in rather a ludicrous way, giving to the dough a process which was a kind of cross between beating and rolling; very uncouth it was but it certainly kneaded the dough.

Then was the thin layer of dough removed, cut into slices with enormous knives,the slices cut into small squares, and each square worked by hand into the circular form of a biscuit. The biscuits were stamped and pierced and thrown dexterously into the mouth of an oven, where they fell upon a flat shovel called a peel, and were transferred from the peel to the floor of the oven. This act of throwing the biscuits into the oven, so as to fall exactly on the right spot, became quite celebrated as an act of skilful sleight of hand.

The completed ship's biscuit was flinty hard and apparently impervious to the jaws of anything short of a biscuit weevil. While the biscuits were standing about waiting to be headed up in casks, or while they were opened aboard ship, they were usually attacked by a particular kind of fly which laid its eggs in the biscuits. Before long, the larvae would begin to emerge in the shape of white grubs. Veteran seamen often tapped a biscuit on the table in the hope of persuading the weevils to emerge and leave it. They did not always oblige.

The bread ration, in Cromwell's time, was a pound and a half, together with a gallon of flour. Sailors would try to make bread for themselves with the flour if the galley cook would oblige. Like the biscuit, the flour too was usually infested with insect life.

DRINK ABOARD SHIP

The worst feature of life aboard ship was the drink. Cromwell had ordered that his sailors should have a gallon of beer a week — a generous allowance, even when it is remembered that there was no other drink available except water.

As brewed during the seventeenth century, beer would not keep for any length of time afloat.* Accordingly, Cromwell canceled the beer ration for his seamen and issued rum instead. Fortunately, large quantities of rum were made available for the Royal Navy with the capture of Jamaica by the English in 1655.

Nobody would willingly drink water aboard ship, because it was kept in casks and invariably became green and slimy after only a short time at sea. Londoners bluffed simple sea captains into believing that Thames water kept better than any other, so many ships must have gone to sea with the contents of a sewer in their water barrels. Much of a sea captain's life was spent looking for a landfall where he could refill his water casks — a long and arduous task which was responsible for the ruptures that invalided so many seamen. All sorts of places became well known to navigators as spots where they could renew their water, St. Helena and the Cape of Good Hope being two examples.

STARVATION AT SEA

The real nightmare of a sea voyage was not being obliged to eat the frightful food aboard ship, but having nothing at all to eat, as the following voyage will show. Colonel Norwood, a Cavalier follower of the exiled Charles II, decided to leave England with two friends, Major Francis Morrison and Major Richard Fox, and emigrate to Virginia. They sailed from the Downs on September 23, 1649, in "the good ship (untruly so called) *The Virginia Merchant*, burden three hundred tons."

Twenty days out from the Downs "our cooper began about this time to complain that our water cask was almost empty, alleging that there was not enough in the hold for our great family (about three hundred and thirty souls) to serve a month."

Luckily Fayal, one of the Azores, was just over the horizon. They were able to renew their water supplies there, but "the second night after we anchored here, our ship's long boat was staved in pieces by the

---

*It was not till the nineteenth century that the brewers devised a beer which would keep in cask for long sea voyages. It became famous as "India Pale Ale," because much of it was sold to the British in India.

seamens' neglect, who had all tasted so liberally of new wine, by the commodiousness of the vintage, that they lay up and down dead drunk in all quarters, in a sad pickle. Getting water was so tedious in itself,'' says Norwood, ''for want of our boat, and so full of delay by drunken contests of our men and the islanders, that after some days stay upon the island, when our Captain resolved to sail away, he found the ship in a worse condition for liquors than when we came on shore, for if we got a new supply of water the proportion was hardly enough to balance the expense of beer that was spent in the time we got it.''

After taking aboard ''store of black pigs for fresh meat,'' and ''peaches without number'' which Norwood had bought for his private stores, the *Virginia Merchant* set sail once more. In a short time she made the Bermudas, but, changing course northward, she was caught in a gale which nearly swept her onto the beaches of Hatteras.

The gale dismasted the ship, carrying away her forecastle (with one of the two cooks).

> Both passengers and seamen were in a deplorable state as to the remaining victuals, ''all like to fall under extreme want, for the storm, by taking away the forecastle, having thrown much water into the hold, our bread (the staff of life) was greatly damnified, and there remained no way to cook our meat, now that the cookroom was gone. The incessant tumbling of the ship made all such cookery wholly impracticable. The only expedient to make fire between decks was by sawing a cask in the middle and filling it with ballast, which made a hearth to parch peas and broil salt beef. Nor could this be done but with great attendance, which was many times frustrated by being thrown topsy turvy in spite of all circumspection, to the great defeat of empty stomachs.

The gale continued to hold, and in spite of valiant efforts to repair the ship, no landfall on the American coast had been made yet, ''our water being long since spent, our meat spoiled or useless, no kind of victuals remaining to sustain life, but a biscuit cake a day for a man, at which allowance there was not a quantity to hold out many days.''

The gale continued to hold.

> The famine grew sharp upon us. Women and children made dismal cries and grievous complaints. The infinite number of rats that all the voyage had been our plague, we now were glad to make our prey to feed on, and as they were insnared and taken, a well grown rat was sold for sixteen shillings as a market rate. Nay, before the voyage did end (as I was

credibly informed) a woman great with child offered twenty shillings for a rat, which the proprietor refusing, the woman died.

Though the crew and passengers of the *Virginia Merchant* were not beginning to drop with famine, what remained of the provisions was not put in a common pool, as Norwood tells us.

> Many sorrowful days and nights we spun out in ths manner, till the blessed feast of Christmas came upon us, which we began with a very melancholy solemnity, and yet, to make some distinction of times, the scrapings of the meal tubs were all amassed together to compose a pudding: Malaga Sack, sea water with fruit and spice, all well fried in oil, were the ingredients of this treat, which raised some envy in the spectators, but allowing some privilege to the Captain's mess, we met no obstruction but did peaceably enjoy our Christmas Pudding.
>
> My greatest impatience was of thirst, and my dreams were all of cellars, and taps running down my throat, which made my waking much the worse by that tantalizing fancy. I found some very real relief by the Captain's favour in allowing me a share of some butts of thin claret he had concealed in a private cellar.

SCURVY

By this time several members of the ship's complement were suffering not merely from starvation, but from what was called the seaman's disease — that is, scurvy. When eventually the *Virginia Merchant* did succeed in anchoring off the American shore, the first care was to take these sick ashore, so that they might recover by eating fresh food.

Scurvy is a disease caused by a deficiency of vitamin C, the vitamin obtained from fresh fruit and vegetables and meat. Almost all animals except man synthesize vitamin C for themselves. They have no need of a diet that occasionally includes fruit or vegetables, because they have enough ascorbic acid, another name for vitamin C, in their bloodstream. Because of this, one way to obtain vitamin C is by eating a freshly slaughtered animal, such as the rats that Colonel Norwood and his companions were eating aboard the *Virginia Merchant*. As has been seen, however, there were never enough rats aboard ship to go round. As a source of vitamin C, early sailors ate citrus fruit, which has a high vitamin-C content. Of course these ancient mariners knew nothing about vitamins, but they knew empirically that a change to a particular kind of diet would cure "the seaman's disease."

Jacques Cartier, icebound at what is now Quebec during the winter of 1535 – 36, saw nine tenths of his men laid out with scurvy — only to recover within a week after drinking an infusion of arborvitae bark. As early as 1601 the sailors of the English East India Company were aware of the connection between eating oranges and lemons and curing scurvy. Anchored off the southernmost cape of Madagascar, they would collect large quantities of oranges and lemons, and squeeze the juice into barrels as an ''antiscorbutic'' or remedy against scurvy.

Lemon juice had been taken up as an antiscorbutic by other seamen besides the English, notably Mediterranean sailors, but it took a very long time for it to be universally adopted. One reason for this was that many people, and in particular doctors, vigorously attacked the idea of eating fruit at all, or drinking fruit juice, as a cure. Some people even attributed the very high death rate on sea voyages to the fact that sailors ate too much tropical fruit when they arrived at their destinations.

So scurvy continued to make terrible ravages amongst the crews of vessels bound on long voyages. In 1619, for example, Jens Munk, a Danish admiral, led an expedition of sixty-four men in two ships to the mouth of the Churchill River in Hudson Bay. The Danes wintered there and remained in reasonably good health during the first months of winter. Then, one by one, they began to fall ill with scurvy. By June only four were still alive; Munk was one of them.

A few green shoots were beginning to push out of the earth in the late Arctic spring, and Munk and his companions sucked them desperately. They could not chew, because scurvy had loosened the teeth in their swollen gums. By means of superhuman effort, Munk and his companions, now reduced to three, were able to get the smaller of their vessels set on a course for Denmark. Scurvy had claimed the other sixty-one explorers.

One of the most unpleasant features of scurvy was that it emphasized the distinction between the ''haves'' and the ''have nots.'' The ''have nots'' would most likely find themselves dying of scurvy, while the ''haves'' were able to remain relatively healthy because they had their own cabin stores. Louis Antoine, Comte de Bougainville (1729 – 1811), set off on a voyage around the world in 1767. It was a voyage which was to have all sorts of important consequences, not the least of them the discovery of bougainvillea, possibly the most beautiful of all tropical flowers. One of the officer who had sailed with Bougainville kept a record of the voyage. The following extracts from his diary will show the painful differences which existed aboard ship between those who, like Bougainville, had laid in special stores, and those who merely relied on the ship's victuals.

> As my journal is intended to benefit my son, I must try to leave out of it nothing from which he might derive some utility. I therefore feel obliged to warn him never to go on board ship for expeditions of this sort (even though he expects to dine at the captain's table) without considerable private stores of drinking chocolate, coffee, and cakes of stock for making broth. The supplies we drew from Tahiti are exhausted. The chickens did not do very well, they refused to eat any of our grain, to which they were unaccustomed, and several of them have died.
>
> In the end, various members of the expedition staff have developed scurvy, and unfortunately I am one of them. My mouth is completely ruined by it. We are unable to relieve ourselves of the disease by eating any kind of fresh meat. I ate a rat with the Prince of Nassau yesterday. We decided that it was very good, and we should be happy if we could have rat often, without other folk deciding that it was good too . . . .
>
> A new kind of ragout was served up at supper. It was made of cooked leather which came from the leather sacks our flour was stored in. By leaving it to soak it is possible to soften the leather somewhat. Then the hair is pulled off. Nonetheless, it is not nearly so good as the rats. Three rats were served up at table today, which were devoured during the dinner
> . . . .
>
> Monsieur de Bougainville has two cooks, a valet, two stewards, and three negroes. I cannot refrain from observing here that if it is hard for the staff officers to see themselves reduced to eating nothing but the ordinary crews' rations, it is even more painful never to see the head of the expedition taking a meal with them, although he ought not to have any other table. He is accustomed to drinking chocolate made with almond paste, sugar, and water, so that is the only addition to his diet, over and above our provisions. I could add that he has also the milk from a goat which he has enjoyed since Montevideo (it is going to be killed today). This subsistence however, added to the other victuals, makes his condition a very different one from ours. He has the proof of it in his face, and he revels in a wonderful roundness of features which puts our thin and starved countenances to shame.

ANTISCORBUTIC DRINKS

Drinking chocolate would not help stave off scurvy, though it might make the fetid water more palatable. Scurvy was to remain a scourge of all deep-water navigators until the eighteenth century, when in 1753 a

Scots naval surgeon named James Lind, after a series of careful experiments, published *A Treatise on the Scurvy*. This study made clear that the disease was caused by a dietary deficiency and could be cured by eating oranges and lemons or drinking their juice.

Little attention was paid to Lind, however, until Captain James Cook (1728 – 79) came along. Cook had begun his sailing career before the mast — something impossible in the French navy — so he was able to talk to seamen in their own language. On his voyages of discovery, he took along casks of lemon juice and sauerkraut and persuaded the men to try it. The result was that not one crew member died of scurvy on any of Cook's three long voyages.

Even so, the Royal Navy did not receive official issues of antiscorbutics until 1795, sixteen years after Cook's death. And it was lime juice in place of lemon (earning British sailors their American nickname ''Limeys''), although lime juice is less effective than other citrus juices.

THE BUCCANEERS

The necessity of long-distance expeditions to stock up with fresh meat gave rise to what is perhaps the strangest episode in the whole story of how food changed history, the Buccaneer era.

Toward the beginning of the seventeenth century, in the islands of the Caribbean, small settlements of non-Spanish European settlers began to go into the business of supplying passing ships with freshly cured meat.

The beef and pork were home-cured according to an old Carib Indian recipe. The Caribs have contributed more words to the English language than any other group of Indians, and ''buccaneer'' is one of them. The buccaneer built a wooden grating out of sticks, which the Caribs called a barbecue, and lighted a wood fire below it. Strips of freshly cut meat were laid out on the grating, and green boughs were fed into the fire to produce lots of smoke but a small amount of flame. The meat dried, smoked, and cooked at the same time, turning into a rose-red piece of preserved meat with a tempting smell. The Caribs called it *boucan*. Boucan had a delicate flavor, and was both nourishing and a cure for scurvy. It was the one item in the ship's stores that even an English cook could not spoil, because it could be eaten raw, chewed like a bar of candy, or softened in water and then cooked in the usual way.

Boucan could be made by salting the meat before it was cut up, or by curing the untreated slices, roughly rubbed in brine, by hanging them in the sun to dry without smoking them over a fire. Smoked meat would keep for several months, but the sun-dried, or charqui, meat had to be eaten fairly quickly. It would turn bad in the damp larder or lazaretto of a ship.

The best-keeping and most delicious boucan was made from the flesh of the wild hog, only the boars being used. Boucan was made up into bundles of a hundred, each of which sold for six "pieces of eight," or about one pound ten shillings of contemporary English money. So you could make a lot of money by becoming a buccaneer, as there were few expenses. All that was needed was the hunting equipment.

Small parties of buccaneers, groups of about seven, would fit themselves out for a hunting expedition. Each carried a special gun with an immense barrel four and a half feet long, with a spade-shaped stock. The buccaneer also carried a blanket and a light tent made of canvas, rolled into a handy size to carry. He had a machete slung at his belt, together with a sailor's knife, and with this he would hack his way through the densely wooded jungle that then covered the Caribbean islands. The buccaneers wore thick leggings and moccasins, with linen trousers and a linen jacket dyed red with the blood of slaughtered animals. This jacket, and the shirt underneath it, were never washed, and the faces of the buccaneers were smeared with grease, all in the hope that these precautions would prevent the mosquitoes attacking them. The jungles of the Caribbean were full of deadly enemies, such as the *fer de lance* or spear-headed pit viper, which hunted people, and the manincheel or poisonous bush, but the only creature which the buccaneers dreaded was the mosquito.

The most interesting piece of equipment of the buccaneer was his cap. This was a contemporary hat with all the brim cut away except for a flap in front, to shade the eyes. It is the ancestor of the modern baseball and jockey caps.

Staggering behind the buccaneers came their servants or valets — really unfortunate white slaves imported from Europe. If they dropped the piles of hides and boucan they carried, or did anything else that their masters objected to, they would be brutally flogged and probably have lemon juice, mixed with salt and red pepper, rubbed into the weals as well.

Almost the only expense of the buccaneer's calling was his powder and shot. He could not afford to miss too often, and he had become so expert that he could hit a coin thrown up into the air. So in their day the buccaneers were probably the most expert marksmen in the world.

Most of the buccaneers were established on the north coast of Haiti and the island of Tortuga — "Turtle Island." Tortuga was their base; here they would buy ammunition, knives, axes, and everything else they needed. When they sighted a Dutch smuggler heading for the Windward Passage, between the easternmost cape of Cuba and the northeast tip of Haiti, they would sail out to her in their little brigantines, confident of being able to sell their smoked meat at a good profit. English and French ships would call at their settlements to take in fresh supplies for the long voyage home. Most of the buccaneers were French or English, but they also numbered Campeche Indians, runaway African slaves, many Dutchmen, and even Irish from Montserrat. The backgrounds of the buccaneers were just as varied as their nationalities. Some were honest men — religious exiles, shipwrecked sailors, and yeomen driven out of the Barbadoes and other islands by sugar. Others were pirates, criminals, deserters, and other bad characters. Yet even if they had been as honest as the day is long, the Spaniards would not have liked them as neighbors on what they regarded as Spanish islands.

In 1638, determined to put an end to the buccaneer problem once and for all, the Spaniards attacked Tortuga and seized whomever they could find. Those who surrendered were hanged. More than three hundred people were massacred in this way, and the hopes of the buccaneers of earning an honest living by supplying boucan to passing ships were dashed for good.

However, most of the Tortuga buccaneers had been out hunting at the time of the raid, and escaped Spanish wrath. They buried their fallen comrades and swore an oath over the graves never to rest till they had avenged them. They now formed themselves into a confederacy called "The Brethren of the Coast."

The idea that a small group of outlaws could successfully engage the vast Spanish Empire, whose proud motto was *"Nec pluribus impar* ("Not unequal to many," implying "A match for the whole world") would have seemed ludicrous to anyone who did not know the Brethren. The buccaneers left nothing to chance. As one who knew them better than most, Alexander Exquemelin, a buccaneer surgeon, wrote: "They are never unprepared." No buccaneer ever let himself get out of reach of his musket and thirty cartridges, his cutlass (the machete of the jungle), and the weapons which were his principal mainstay — his pistols.

Because they knew that, out on the savannah, they would be no match for the splendid Spanish cavalry, the Brethren of the Coast decided to attack the Spaniards at sea. They sailed at first in dugout canoes bought from the Campeche Indians and in tiny brigantines. Such small craft would be almost invisible in a failing light, and in them they could easily creep alongside a small Spanish coaster without being perceived. Once within range, the best shots, who had been lying like the rest on the bottom of the canoe so as not to make too conspicuous a moving object, would rise and pick off the steersman and the watch on deck. Before the rest of the hands could muster from below, the canoe would scrape alongside the coaster, and a wave of boarders would carry her in a rush, firing the several loaded pistols each man carried. The coaster, under buccaneer colors, would then sail in search of larger game.

Exquemelin has described for us a typical buccaneer engagement. As there is a surgeon in this story he may have played a part in it himself and be modestly concealing his own involvement in the affair.

The vice-admiral of a Spanish flotilla had become detached from the rest of his convoy when the watch on deck reported a small craft in the offing, with the warning that she was probably a buccaneer. The don replied contemptuously that nobody would be afraid of a craft that size.

Rightly suspecting that the vice-admiral was too confident to keep a proper watch aboard his flagship, the buccaneer captain kept her within sight till nightfall. He then called his men together (all twenty-eight of them) and reminded them that food was running short. Their own craft was so unseaworthy that she might founder at any moment, but a way existed out this predicament. They would capture the Spanish galleon and share the treasure that she was undoubtedly carrying. The buccaneers enthusiastically swore that they would follow him and do their best. Just in case any of them had second thoughts, the captain ordered the surgeon to sink the ship the moment the boarding party left the deck.

The buccaneers climbed noiselessly aboard the galleon and within a minute or so surprised the captain and his officers playing cards in the cabin. At the point of a pistol the vice-admiral surrendered his craft.

The loot captured aboard a ship of this sort would be sufficient to make every man of the twenty-eight millionaires several times over. One Spanish galleon, the *Santa Margarita,* which was sunk off Key West in 1622 at the height of the buccaneer era, recently yielded $13,920,000 million worth of treasure. A newly captured galleon would be even more valuable than that, since it would contain all sorts of valuable perishables as well as bullion and jewels. Some buccaneers who had captured a cargo of drinking chocolate, for example, threw it overboard under the impression that it was horse dung.

The lure of loot was an incentive against which Spanish bravery was unavailing. In 1668, as a climax to the buccaneer era, Henry Morgan sacked Panama. "If our number is small," he told his men, "our hearts are great, and the fewer of us who survive the attack, the easier it will be to share out the spoils — and the bigger shares we will all get."

Henry Morgan was the last of the buccaneers. Eventually he wangled himself a royal pardon, a knighthood, and a lieutenant governorship of Jamaica. He never returned to his native Wales but settled down at Port Royal to drink himself to death with rum. Power in the Caribbean passed from the hands of the Brethren of the Coast into those of the regular navies of France and England, which arrived to secure their hold on the sugar islands. Those of the Brethren who were unable to accomodate themselves to the change from continuous warfare against the Spaniards to comparative peace sailed off into the sunrise, to find a new career as pirates on the coasts of Madagascar and India.

It is very difficult to assess what were the effects of the buccaneering era. To the Spaniards the consequences of the advent of the men whom they called "the devils from hell," was, of course wholly disastrous. One can sympathize with the Spanish point of view, especially when one reads some of Exquemelin's accounts of Pedro the Brazilian, who used to roam the streets of Jamaica, mad drunk, chopping off the arms and legs of innocent passersby; of the surgeon's former employer, who would plant a cask of wine in the middle of the street, broach it, and force everyone who passed to drink with the alternative of being pistoled on the spot; of other friends of his who fried women naked on hot stones, or fought alligators underwater with a knife, or tortured prisoners to reveal where their treasures were hidden.

Perhaps the real result of the advent of the buccaneers was not what happened in history, but what did not happen. As the Brethren of the Coast dealt body blows at the center of the Spanish octopus, the Caribbean, the tentacles fell back to protect its most vital spots. They did not reach out, as many feared that they might, to the several infant colonies along the North American coast.

7.

Food From The Americas

AMERICA — A LAND OF PLENTY

For the colonists who now began to sail in the wake of the first discoverers, the new-found lands of the Americas represented an end to the centuries-old specter of Europe — hunger. It was true that for the first few years of settlement the new arrivals had to tighten their belts. The English in Virginia were forced to boil into soup the mastiff dogs that they had brought with them to protect them from the Indians while the Pilgrim Fathers needed all their faith to sustain them during the initial winters of the settlement.

Once established, however, colonists in both North and South America found they had come to a land of plenty. The Spaniards in the West Indies discovered that just a small plot of land would support a family throughout the year, so rich were the tropical soils, so suitable for growing food crops were the rains and sunshine of the Caribbean.

They introduced oranges and lemons, grapes, and, most important of all, the sugar cane, brought to the West Indies in 1506. Sheep did not thrive in Central America, but cattle and pigs did. Soon great herds of wild cattle and pigs roamed on the islands, animals which were destined to become the stock in trade of the buccaneers.

Meanwhile the Spaniards hastened to tap the food riches of the new continent. They exported to Spain American vegetables such as cassava, French beans, lima beans, red and green peppers, tapioca, pineapples, peanuts, and vanilla. Yet curiously enough the colonists of Spanish America never learned the most important lessons that the new continent could have taught them.

INSURANCE AGAINST FAMINE

Bernal Diaz, one of the Spanish conquistadores of Mexico, was a practical man of affairs and an agriculturist as well as a soldier, unlike most of his comrades. During an early reconnaissance of Mexico he had even planted some orange pips from an orange he had been eating, and on his return with Cortes, he was delighted to find that the Aztecs, who were keen gardeners like himself, had recognized the shoots of the orange seedlings as a new plant and carefully watered them. At the end of his long life, Diaz was saddened to see the great welfare insurance system of the Aztec emperors completely shattered.

This had consisted in vast storehouses, found in every province and filled with the "taxes" of the emperors' subjects. These taxes, paid in food such as corn, had been saved for a time of disastrous harvest. When famine threatened, the Aztec monarchs would throw open the storehouses, and food would be distributed to the people, so that they could live to sow their seed corn for the following year.

It was the same story in Peru. Everybody ate, but everybody worked, and the connection between working and eating was firmly inculcated into every Peruvian from his childhood on. There were no crowds of beggars as there were in Europe, because nobody was allowed to be idle. All worked for the good of the community as a whole, and the good years of abundant harvests, stored away in the form of extra taxes, paid for the bad years of famine.

The lessons that could have been drawn from the example of the Aztecs and Incas were quite thrown away on the Spaniards, just as, farther north, the Pilgrim Fathers and their descendants could find little to admire in the abundant hospitality of the Indian, who set food before anyone who dropped in to visit him, and where the mighty hunters of the tribe supported, without a murmur, the aged, the orphan, the invalid, and the shiftless.

INDIAN DIET

Most of the Plains and Woodland Indians, like most hunting peoples, lived on a subsistence economy — feasting when there was plenty, fasting when there wasn't. When conditions were favorable — game plentiful, and weather just right — they enjoyed a richer and more abundant diet than any save the richest could afford in Europe. In spring, Northeastern tribes tapped the sugar maple and boiled down the sap, eating the sugar as it crystalized. In summer they hunted or fished, supplementing their meat diet with the corn, squash, and beans raised by their women. In fall they hunted to lay in meat for the lean months of winter, drying bear or buffalo meat over wooden frameworks (much like the barbecues of the buccaneers). This dried and smoked meat was then pounded into shreds, mixed with animal fat to which berries were added, and molded into pemmican. For conditions were not always favorable, and when game disappeared and winter hung on too long, famine would threaten. The the pemmican — containing fat for warmth, meat for protein, and berries for vitamins — kept them alive until the earth turned green again.

It was small wonder that, with a diet so rich in protein Indians should be markedly taller and healthier than their white counterparts. The Pilgrim Fathers soon adopted many of the items on the Indian menu. Turkey, cranberry sauce, corn relish, squash, beans — all the ingredients of the traditional Thanksgiving feast are of Indian origin. So are potatoes, johnnycake (or journeycake), pone, hominy, succotash, and popcorn. All quickly became part of the colonists' way of life.

Though the social classes of "haves" and "have nots" soon reappeared in North America, the poor were never so poor or so hungry as they had been in England. Later, when the fathers of the American Revolution wanted to whip up the mob in America, they were unable to use the standing grievance that inflamed political rioters in eighteenth-century England — the high price of food. They had to fall back on stamp taxes and trade restrictions instead.

AMERICAN FOODS IN EUROPE

The two principal food importations brought from America to Europe had limited success at first. Corn was adopted as a staple crop in Spain, Portugal, and Italy. American Indians, who revered corn, never ate it alone but used it to supplement a meat diet or cooked it with beans, green peppers, and fish — the original form of succotash. These additional items of diet supplied the vitamins lacking in corn. The poorer Europeans, who ate corn as they ate the higher-in-protein wheat — without a meat accompaniment — soon came to suffer from pellagra, "rough skin," a disease caused by protein deficiency.

Corn became unpopular. In 1847 even the starving Irish refused to eat it, calling it "Peel's brimstone," because it was yellow like sulfur, and Peel was Prime Minister of England. In fact, corn remained under a cloud in Europe until Europeans began to adopt the American habit of eating breakfast cereals.

The American* food crop that was going to be taken to the European bosom most thoroughly was, of course, the potato. In 1564 John Hawkins introduced the sweet potato to England, but it never caught on. The Andean potato, on the other hand, which had been cultivated by the industrious Inca farmers on their chilly heights, was an almost instant success. Introduced by Sir Walter Raleigh in 1586 to England, and to England's newly developed colony of Ireland, the potato was to have a great future ahead of it in the British Isles — until the mid-nineteenth century. But that comes later.

Actually, Britain and the potato do not really suit one another. By comparison with Peru, Britain is so warm that the only way to procure seed potatoes is to grow them in the coldest parts of the British Isles, the north of Ireland and Scotland. Because it is growing in a much warmer climate than Nature ever intended for it, the British potato is liable to diseases that would probably never have affected it on the high Andean plateau. Moreover, the Incas, who had originated potato culture, had also developed an absolutely foolproof method of freeze-drying the potato by turning it into *chuñu*.

EUROPEAN ACCEPTANCE OF THE POTATO

There were obviously good agricultural reasons for looking twice at potatoes before adopting them, and their acceptance by European peasants, traditionally obstinate and prejudiced anyway, was slow. In France, Antoine-Auguste Parmentier, an eighteenth-century French *philosophe* (and the purported inventor of "French fries"), tried to

---

* South American, that is. The potato was not introduced into North America until 1719 — from, of all places, Ireland.

convince his countrymen that the potato was not poisonous. (Green, shooting potatoes *are* poisonous to a certain extent, of course.) Parmentier did manage to interest the King, however, and it was Louis XVI who finally tricked the peasantry into trying the new vegetable. He had a field of potatoes planted just outside Paris and set a guard of soldiers around this royal field. Curious peasants wondered what the valuable crop was that needed such tight security. Finally, when his crop was ready, the King withdrew his guard at night — and waited. Before long, every potato had been dug up surreptitiously and carried off, and the *pomme de terre* was on its way. To this day *parmentier* or *à la parmentier* on a French menu means "served with potatoes."

The potato arrived in France just too late to prevent the French Revolution. If, when the crops failed in 1788, the peasants had had a reserve of potatoes to fall back on, if Marie Antoinette* had been able to say, "If they have no bread, let them eat potatoes" then history might have been very different.

Elsewhere in Europe the potato fared better. Frederick the Great introduced it into Germany, where it was such a hit that the War of the Bavarian Succession (1778 – 79) hinged entirely on who controlled the local potato crop. Russians caught the fever and found that the vegetable thrived in their chilly climate. In Holland today, four out of every five vegetables grown are potatoes.

CHOCOLATE

One other American food really took Europe by storm, and this was chocolate.

Like coffee and tea, chocolate is a stimulant, having as its active ingredient a substance called theobromine, which means "food of the gods." This was a much more accurate description than many in botany, because in Aztec Mexico, where it was first seen by Europeans, cocoa was a favorite drink of the emperors, who were regarded as gods by their subjects. The first European to drink chocolate, Cortez, was served it by Montezuma, who offered it to his guest in a golden calabash.

To make chocolate, the Mexicans collected the fruit of the cacao tree, which is an evergreen with yellow roselike flowers and drooping bright

*Actually she didn't. This remark first appeared in print in Rousseau's *Confessions* in 1766, while Marie was a child of eleven still living in Austria. And even Rousseau seems to have been quoting an old proverb with the sense, "Well, we must put up with misfortunes as best we can." It was foisted on the queen by Revolutionary propagandists.

green leaves, split open the fruits and exposed them to the sun until they "sweat." They next ground the pods on a stone grinder called a *metatl*. Thomas Gage, an Englishman who was to have much to do with chocolate, assures us that the name comes from *choco-choco,* an onomatopoeic word imitating the sound of the swishing chocolate in the water, and *atle,* the name of the grinder.

Chocolate was so expensive that it could hardly have been the drink of poor peasants. It was used in Mexico as a currency instead of the coinage that the Aztecs had never originated. The pods of cacao were made up into packs of 24,000 pods as a standard unit of currency. With these packs, the Mexicans and the Mayas paid their taxes.

As drunk by Montezuma and Cortez, chocolate was a cold delicacy, not liquid, but frothed to a thick consistency like that of honey, so that it had to be eaten with a spoon. It was mixed with all sorts of spices, including one which is still added to chocolate, vanilla. The Aztecs often added ground corn to their chocolate.

In European hands, chocolate changed considerably. It became a drink, not a food, because it was so expensive that it had to be watered down. But it was still frothed, and a variety of spices were still added to it, every drinker having his own formula.

As taken by the Aztecs, it had probably included several natural aphrodisiacs. Chocolate continued to be regarded as an aphrodisiac by both the English and the French. It is characteristic of the two national temperaments that whereas the French drank chocolate freely, they worried about drinking coffee because their doctors assured them it would make them impotent, and the English, unworried about coffee, were concerned over the effects of chocolate on women's chastity (*men's* chastity was not considered nearly so important).

By the end of the eighteenth century, chocolate was no longer considered to be dangerous to female virtue. It was widely drunk all over Europe, and it was one of the drinks which made possible the European intellectual revolution known as the Enlightenment. Ladies of rank and fashion in France would give parties, called *salons.* Here chocolate or coffee would be served to the company, who were all men except the hostess and all intellectuals. As they drank their chocolate, they would discuss the burning questions of the day — such as whether the powers of the French King should be limited, as were those of the King of England, and what could be done to improve the lot of the peasantry.

Chocolate had so completely lost its daring reputation that it was widely drunk by schoolgirls and nuns. One such chocolate lover was

Madame d'Arestrel, superior of the Convent of the Visitation, at Belley, who had a young friend named Anselme Brillat-Savarin. The French Revolution was shortly to drive Anselme from France to New York, where he kept body and soul together by playing in a theater orchestra, but he must have already been contemplating his great work on gastronomy, because he noted down the recipe the mother superior gave him for making good chocolate.

"Make it before hand in a porcelain chocolate pot the night before you want to drink it," said Madame d'Arestrel, "then leave it all night. By resting through the night, it acquires a concentration and velvety texture which makes it infinitely enhanced. The good Lord will not grudge us this little refinement, for is he not Himself all perfection?"

8.

The Saga Of Sugar

INCREASED CONSUMPTION

Sugar has been mentioned in this book so many times already that the reader might well ask, what could there be about it that was revolutionary? It had been introduced to the Mediterranean world by Darius, King of Persia, from India, after his conquests there. What was there about sugar at the end of the sixteenth century that was new?

The answer lies in the quantities of sugar consumed. In the Middle Ages it had been a very exotic commodity indeed, recommended by doctors to their patients on account of its health-giving qualities. By the middle of the nineteenth century, it was no longer the preserve of kings or princes but was eaten by everyone in Europe and America, even paupers. In 1847 a Poor Law inspector in Yorkshire, England, complained about "the large quantity of wine and sugar given to the outdoor sick under the direction of the medical officers."

Like the spices, sugar has no dietetic value whatsoever. It is merely a carbohydrate source of energy; once the energy has been used up, we are none the better for having eaten the sugar. The energy obtained could just as easily have been acquired from any other energy-giving food carbohydrate or protein. Too much sugar consumption does produce obesity — a fact which was discovered as early as the eighteenth century by poultrymen, who found that nothing fattened fowls more quickly for the market than a sugar diet. Obesity can in turn produce heart disease. Sugar left on the teeth can cause decay.

Because sugar is not necessary to support life, the struggles and strivings that are characteristic of the Sugar Revolution may seem so much labor spent in vain. It should not be forgotten, though, that the desire to eat is psychological, not physiological. Although some food tastes change, the desire for sugar has not. Twelve million tons a year are consumed in the United States, and in Britain, no less than 120 pounds per head a year.

At the end of the sixteenth century all sugar, apart from what the Indians of North America obtained from the sugar maple, was derived from the sugar cane.

GROWING AND REFINING SUGAR

Growing, harvesting, and processing sugar was not an easy business, as a few words quoted from the seventeenth century French writer, Louis Moreri, will show:

> Sugar is formed from a juice which by its nature moistens the spongy pith of certain reeds or canes, which grow in abundance on this island, and in several others nearby. Sugar cane also grows on the mainland of America but its juice is not nearly so finely flavored as the West Indian variety, nor is that which is produced in some of the islands of Asia.
>
> The sugar canes are scarcely higher than six feet, and are two inches thick. Those which are nearly as thick as one's arm are not so good. The canes have nodes every six inches along the stem. To plant cane, small cuttings are placed in well-tilled ground. At the end of six to seven months, they come to maturity, and their ripeness can be seen from the color, a sort of golden yellow.
>
> This indicates that it is time to cut them, and when this is done, and their leaves lopped, the canes are tied in bundles and taken to the press. Sugar mills consist of three sets of rollers. While these turn, Negro slaves throw cane into the gap between them. The rollers crush the cane and throw it out onto the other side. The juice from the canes drains into a large tank below and from there, by means of a little gutter, it pours off into a big cauldron. Beneath this cauldron a slow fire is kept burning so as to heat up the sugar and send the scum to the surface without making it boil. From this cauldron it is ladled into another where it is made to boil

and bubble by means of a hotter fire, the better to raise the skimmings to the surface where they can be scummed off.

Once the sugar can be seen to be getting thick it is filtered through linen, then shared out into several smaller coppers, where it is boiled while being continually stirred, till it is completely cooked. This stage can be seen to have arrived once the sugar, on being poured out, flows thickly and consistently. At this point it is allowed to cool in the small coppers, which continue to be stirred, till the grains of sugar, like grains of sand, appear in the syrup. This is the sign that the process is now complete. Thereupon the syrup is poured into molds shaped like pyramids. Once the sugar is congealed, and solid, clay mixed with water is poured into the sugar shapes. It drains off at the bottom, carrying with it an amber-colored residue of the sugar.

The very hard work required to make a sugar plantation conditioned the whole society of the sugar islands — just as the very easy work needed to grow enough potatoes to live on conditioned life in Ireland. Sugar-cane growing had been started on the American continent by the first Spanish settlers. In Mexico, the sugar cane had been introduced by Hernando Cortez as early as 1530. The Caribbean provided sugar with just the kind of climate it required, a climate much more suitable than that of its native land, India, because there was much more rain. It flourished so well that in 1520 there were no fewer than sixty sugar factories on the island of St. Thomas alone. Meanwhile on the South American mainland, in Brazil, the Portuguese also set up sugar plantations, which also flourished.

SUGAR AND SLAVERY

A great difficulty soon made itself felt about the labor force, however. No Spaniard would do any work for himself if he could get someone to do it for him, not out of sheer laziness but because Spanish society looked down on the ordinary tiller of the fields.

So the Spaniards set the native inhabitants of the Caribbean to work for them. On the Greater Antilles, where a great deal of sugar planting now began, there lived two principal groups of Indians, the Caribs and the Arawaks. The Arawaks were a gentle people who allowed themselves to be rounded up by the Spanish conquistadors and driven off to the cane fields. There they were worked to death. If they attempted to escape into the jungle, the Spaniards hunted them down with bloodhounds imported from England, and inflicted terrible punishment on them. Soon the Arawaks had become completely extinct.

That left the Caribs. They were made of sterner stuff, and they resisted the Spaniards determinedly with their wooden clubs, called *boutous*, and with arrows tipped with a deadly poison. Soon the Caribs were either exterminated or driven to remote and rocky islands where it would be unprofitable to start sugar plantations.

The Spaniards now had to look elsewhere for a labor force, and they cast an eye on the possessions of Portugal (which had become part of Spain from the sixteenth to the seventeenth centuries). The Portuguese had not worked their Indian subjects in Brazil into the ground in order to produce sugar. Realizing that the Indians were not able to stand the rigors of regular hard daily work because they had never been used to it, they began to import African slaves from the Portuguese colonies in West and East Africa. The Africans were hard workers, they were used to life in a tropical climate, and they had natural resistance to many tropical diseases such as hookworm and malaria. They were just the sort of people to provide an efficient labor force in the cane fields. Cane growing was a complex business demanding careful preparation of the soil, hoeing and weeding, slashing, and, at the end, immense labor in a very short space of time, as every piece of cut cane had to be transported from the field to the crusher before it spoiled — a period of just twenty-four hours.

Above all, slaves were cheap. Slavery had existed in Africa from the earliest times and originally most slaves were prisoners who had been taken in tribal wars or debtors who had defaulted, and by the practice of "panyaring," had become the property of their creditors. Others had committed minor offenses, or were people who were disliked by the chief for some reason or other. Slaves were a superfluous luxury to an African chief, because if he wanted any work done, the whole tribe would turn out to do it for him. The only real use for slaves was in human sacrifices, and in places such as Dahomey, many of them were sacrificed to fetishes. So, most chiefs were prepared to sell their slaves for guns, ammunition, cloth, wire, glass beads, and rum — a by-product of sugar which we will discuss presently.

Because the Spaniards and the Portuguese had begun to develop their sugar plantations with slave labor from Africa, everyone else felt that they had to follow their example, otherwise the sugar that they produced would cost more and be priced out of the market. This was ironic, since the original settlers of the Caribbean had often been idealistic

Frenchmen and Englishmen, sometimes religious refugees, sometimes high-principled individuals who wished to live a freer life than was possible in Europe. They had not meant to own slaves. What they had wanted to do was farm their own land as smallholders. They had envisaged growing ginger, indigo (a dye for textiles), cotton, and particularly tobacco, which had indeed became a well-paying crop on many islands.

The inducements to grow sugar, however, were almost overwhelming. Dutch entrepreneurs brought sugar cane from Brazil (temporarily in the hands of the Dutch) to Barbadoes, showed the English settlers how to plant it, when to harvest it, how to set up a sugar crusher, and how to refine the liquid sugar. The Dutch were even prepared to lend the English planters sugar-crushing equipment on credit against the value of the sugar to be produced. The first sugar factory in the English New World opened at Barbadoes in 1641. Twenty years later the whole island was covered by sugar estates, and most of the original white smallholders had left, dispossessed by "subtle and greedy planters." Their places in the fields were taken by black slaves, and the same process was effected in all the Caribbean islands. Some of the white yeoman farmers went north to the mainland colonies, but others joined the fleets of the buccaneers, which were forming.

THE DEMON RUM

Why should sugar growing have suddenly become so prosperous? One reason is those residues from the sugar-distillation process which had formerly been poured off. It had now been discovered that they were the raw material for a new kind of liquor, rum.

Distilled liquors had been known about for centuries but they only came into prominence at the time of the Sugar Revolution. Ancient India and China had had their stills for the production of toddy and arrack, and when the first invasion of Ireland by the English took place, in 1170– 72, the Irish were already distilling whiskey. Records of distillation in Scotland are scanty, but scotch may be almost as old as Irish whiskey, and Arnold of Villanova had begun to distill brandy from wine in France in the thirteenth century. Still spirit drinking had only become important during the sixteenth century. There is good reason to regard rum as the first mass-produced spirit. Unlike the raw materials for brandy (wine) or whiskey (grain), molasses, the basis of rum, cost nothing — it was an unwanted by-product.

"Rumbullion" is a Devon word meaning "tumult," and it was soon shortened to rum. The other name for the drink, "Kill Devil," was long popular in New England and can still be heard occasionally in New-foundland. "The chief fuddling they make in the island," wrote an inhabitant of Barbadoes in 1651, "is Rumbullion, alias Kill Devil, and this is made of sugar canes distilled, a hot, hellish and terrible liquor."

To make rum, the residues of the sugar-making process — liquid drainings from the sugar loaf molds and solid skimmings from the cauldrons — were mixed with molasses, fermented, and distilled. So everything that came from the sugar cane was used up and turned to the planters' profit.

Rum soon became a standard issue in the Royal Navy, as well as the Army, issued regularly to British sailors from 1688 on. It was intended as a substitute for the beer which had previously been served aboard ship, since beer did not travel well. Rum, stored in casks, kept very well aboard ship. The original rum issue had been half a pint per man per day. As the liquor was 96 proof, the equivalent of six double whiskeys, Admiral Vernon started the practice of diluting the rum with twice its volume of water before it was served out to the men — the famous grog. The rum issue was one of the few bright spots in the sailor's or soldier's day.

The strength of rum made it very desirable as trade goods, too, and it became a standard item for all diplomatic exchanges with savages. When for example "Corlaer," the Iroquois name for whoever was governor of New York Colony, met the Indians in counsel, barrels of rum were always demanded as a gift and were always forthcoming.

SUGAR IN TEA, COFFEE, AND CHOCOLATE

There was another reason for the sudden popularity of sugar in Europe. It was being used, more and more, to sweeten the new drinks that had risen in favor during the seventeenth century — tea, coffee, and chocolate.

Though these three drinks had had very different histories, they all became important to Europeans at about the same time, the seventeenth century, just when the big demand for sugar began. It is curious to note that none of them had been sweetened in the countries that gave them birth, but the moment they were introduced to Europe, consumers began to sweeten them lavishly with sugar. They also added milk or cream, and they made all three drinks much stronger than they were prepared in the countries of origin.

This altered use pattern was partly caused by the availability of the materials added to them. The Chinese, for example, had no milk or cream to add to their tea. They had almost no pasture, and the only bovines they kept were buffalo for plowing. Besides, they have always disliked the smell of milk products (they say cheese smells like corpses), and the only place where you cold buy cheese or milk in a Chinese city was in the special restaurants kept for Mongols or Tartars. (The Chinese have had to pay heavily for this food faddiness; they have been frequently invaded by the hardy horsemen of the steppes, who were nourished on a diet of milk and cheese.)

As for sugar, although it had been known long before the seventeenth century, it had never before been available in such large quantities. Moreover, English people, who were to be the most enthusiastic pioneers of the new drinks at their outset, have always had a sweet tooth — in the fifteenth century the Venetian ambassador had been amazed to see them stirring spoonfuls of sugar even into their wine — and the English set the pattern.

TEA

Of the three drinks, tea had the oldest history, and perhaps the strangest as well. It had been discovered by an amateur herb doctor looking for new remedies. In 2737 B.C. the Chinese Emperor Shen Nung was preparing himself a herbal tisane outdoors. He placed a kettle of water on a fire under a *Camellia thea* tree, and leaves from the tree fell into the boiling water. It must have been a mild autumn because the leaves had dried on the tree, and before Shen Nung could get them out of the cauldron, they had filled it with an infusion of such fragrance that the Emperor just had to try a sip to see what it was like.

As an amateur physician, Shen Nung naturally tried out his new discovery. He soon found that tea would not cure any diseases, but it could be used in medicine to produce perspiration, which was useful in certain treatments. There was also one condition of suffering humanity which it really did ease — fatigue. One sip helped very much with the business of waking up and rising in the morning, or helped the tea drinker to work far into the night without dropping off over his state papers. Tea promoted wakefulness because it is a stimulant. It contains theine, an alkaloid stimulant, which is closely allied to the theobromine of chocolate and the caffeine of coffee.

Tea was enthusiastically adopted in China as the drink of the nobility, the Buddhist clergy, and the intellectuals. Only much later did it become the drink of the common people, who cultivated it. Tea went through three ages. In the first age it was compressed into a "brick" or cake of tea, of the kind still made in China for sale among the Tibetans and Tartars. Bricks of this sort are marked off into grooves on one side so that they can be broken up into smaller pieces for use. A cube of tea would be broken off, pounded in a mortar, and then boiled with the water along with strange-sounding ingredients such as rice, ginger, salt, orange peel, pine kernels, milk, walnuts, and even onions. The only relic left of this early method of preparing tea is the slice of lemon which we still often squeeze into the infusion.

Then the fashion changed, and leaf tea was powdered into fine dust, and mixed into a sort of soup with warm, instead of boiling water. It was at this stage of evolution of tea that it reached Japan, and the Japanese have kept up this method of preparing it in the tea ceremony, an elaborate ritual which is a sort of school of polite manners.

In the sixteenth century the first tea pots appeared as a new method of making tea was introduced, infusing the crumbled leaves in a tea pot with boiling water. It was at this stage of its development, in 1610, that tea first reached Europe aboard a Dutch ship.

To begin with, the influence of tea on European life was very limited, because only small amounts of the finest teas were imported. Gradually, though, English potters were called on to imitate the tea pots and tea cups which were imported from China, thus stimulating the rise of English pottery and porcelain factories.

Before the arrival of tea, everyone in England had drunk beer, and nothing but beer, because there was nothing else to drink. No one would have thought of drinking the water, which was almost always contaminated and unhealthy. The rise of the tea-drinking habit meant that now children could be given nonalcoholic drinks for the first time. Moreover the water from which tea was made was boiled, thus killing the bacteria it certainly contained when it went into the kettle.

Moralists such as William Cobbett lamented the days when every Englishman made his own beer and drank nothing else throughout the year. Cobbett complained that not merely was tea debilitating for working-class folk, it was a taste that was above their station. They just could not afford it. Cobbett produced a number of figures to prove how much it cost to drink beer, and how expensive it was to drink tea. Tea was expensive during the eighteenth century, when it began to be drunk by consumers of all classes in England. Yet the need to buy this expensive beverage — which cost one pound sterling a pound — helped to promote the rise of an industrial work force, that had learned that the higher wages they could earn in the new factories would enable them to buy luxuries like tea.

COFFEE

Before 1650 coffee had been drunk only by European travelers abroad. It had apparently originated in Ethiopia, probably in the district of Kafia, and had been first drunk by a monk who noticed that goats that browsed on the coffee tree skipped wildly about, endued with energy and wakefulness. The Great Italian traveler Pietro della Valla commented, "It prevents those who consume it from feeling drowsy; for that reason students who wish to read into the late hours are fond of it."

Coffee drinking was introduced into England by the Greek Orthodox Bishop of Smyrna, who was visiting Oxford. John Evelyn, an undergraduate, looked on in wonder in 1637 as the bishop went through the ritual of making, then drinking, coffee. In 1650 the first commercial coffeehouse in Europe opened its doors, in Oxford. No doubt the reputation of coffee as a drink which enabled students to burn the midnight oil helped to promote the sale of the new, exotic, beverage. By 1699 the English were the prime consumers of coffee in the Western world. "This drink," wrote Louis Moreri, in 1699, "has become very fashionable in Europe, above all England and France. It is said that just in the town of London there are three thousand 'Caffez' or houses set aside for drinking this beverage, and they are full of drinkers all day, and a part of the night."

The patrons of the coffeehouses may have come in for coffee, but they stayed for a chat. Coffee was the magic key that unlocked the lips of the usually taciturn Englishman. The coffeehouses became not merely restaurants but clubs.

COFFEEHOUSES

The coffeehouse was a rather austere room, with a bar at one end. At the bar sat a very ladylike young woman, fashionably dressed in the style of the day, dispensing tea and coffee in bowls (not cups). Her presence set restraints to the speech, and behavior, of the customers. Boys would scurry around from the bar, filling the customers' orders and also taking the copies of the various newspapers, for the coffeehouse provided free journals.

Soon coffee drinkers of a particular calling began to frequent one particular coffeehouse. Clergymen, for example, tended to drop in to the Cocoa Tree, in Covent Garden. Actors, such as Garrick, could be found at the Bedford, near the theaters. Many businessmen patronized Lloyd's Coffee House, which eventually stopped selling coffee and became the first modern insurance agency, as well as a bank.

Rather belatedly the coffee habit crossed the Channel. French doctors warned their patients that coffee drinking was the road to ruin. When a coffeehouse opened in Marseilles, toward the end of the seventeenth century, the town physicians held a public meeting to explain to the townspeople just how pernicious a drink coffee was. The eastern brew, said a Dr. Colomb, was a hot and very dry substance, which deprived the body of its natural juices, plaguing the drinker with eternal wakefulness, exhaustion, and impotence.

Frenchmen began to doubt the wisdom of their doctors when it became evident that in spite of the incrimination of coffee as a killer, it had certainly not killed off the English. Between 1680 and 1730 more coffee was consumed in London alone than anywhere else in the world. One French convert to coffee was a very influential one — Voltaire. He had been forced to spend some time in exile in England because of his outspoken attacks on the Church and the government in France, and had come back with an admiration for English coffeehouses and coffee. When in later life he was told by an abbé to beware of coffee because it was a poison, the great *philosophe* remarked caustically that it was the slowest poison on record. He had been drinking it for fifty years and it had not killed him yet!

SUGAR AND THE FRENCH ECONOMY

We can see how important sugar had become to the European economy by looking at a few trade figures from France at the end of the eighteenth century. By that time thousands of Frenchmen owed their livelihood to the sugar imports which reached France from her plantations in the Antilles. Paris, Rouen, Nantes, La Rochelle, and Bordeaux had become important industrial towns largely because of the sugar industry. The Bordeaux refineries produced one fifth of the total sugar consumed in Europe. France was the biggest importer of sugar in the world. Her consumption kept on going up and up during the eighteenth century, so that by 1789, she was importing 140,000 tons, forty thousand more than her rival in the sugar trade, England, imported. After refining the raw-sugar imports, France sold much of her refined output to Amsterdam, the Hanseatic towns, Germany, and Scandinavia.

Obviously sugar was very much the lifeblood of French industry, and if any other European country interfered with her sugar trade, it would earn the undying enmity of the French — this is just what did happen, as we shall see.

WHITE AND BLACK SLAVES

In an attempt to deal with the ever-growing demand for sugar from coffee and chocolate drinkers in Europe, French and British planters tried to solve their labor problems by importing white slaves. These were prisoners of war (such as the Royalist Cavaliers whom Cromwell shipped to Barbadoes, and whose descendants still live there), petty criminals, or unfortunates who could be kidnapped and sold into slavery without anyone raising a finger.

Technically, the white slaves were not slaves but indentured servants, as there was no legal recognition of slavery in England, by English law. The indentured servants were supposed to be released from their masters' clutches at the end of five years and be given an outfit sufficient to enable them to set up as planters for themselves. Many of them never saw the end of their indentures. One planter baked his indentured servants alive in ovens, another systematically starved them to death, and then rubbed a little white of egg on their lips as they lay dying, so that he could swear in court, if need be, that he had forced food on them to the last.

There were never enough white slaves to go round, and the surplus had to be made good from Africa. Instead of merely collecting the prisoners of tribal wars, the slave traders now began to foment wars between chiefs and carry off whole tribes into captivity. Bands of slave traders began to undertake raids into the interior in search of slaves. During the whole of the slave trade, from the sixteenth to the early nineteenth century twenty million black men, women, and children were carried overseas, of whom two thirds were sent to the plantations in the West Indies, Brazil, or America. They were not all employed in growing sugar — other crops such as indigo were grown as well — but sugar growing was very much the prop of the whole plantation system in the West Indies.

The results of the growth of the sugar industry were almost wholly evil so far as Africa was concerned. There was great loss of life, the authority of the chiefs declined, tribes were broken up and families dispersed. In some areas cultivation ceased almost entirely, and African arts and crafts went into a decline.

The slave trade also had some minor benefits for Africa. Many of the food plants which now seem indigenous to the African shamba (bananas and corn, for example) were in fact imports introduced by the slave traders. More important, the African problem now became of concern to Europeans.

ANTISLAVERY MOVEMENT

Nowhere was concern for Africans — and particularly those uprooted from their homes by the slave trade — felt more keenly than in England, and this was justifiable because England had taken a leading part in the trade.

Groups of religiously minded men, particularly the "New Dissenting" sects such as the Methodists, now began a vigorous campaign to abolish slavery and the slave trade. Hand in hand with this program went a desire to better the lot of the Africans by sending out missionaries who would not merely evangelize them, but help them develop better methods of agriculture and commerce which would replace the one real trade in Africa, the slave trade.

Prominent in this attack on slavery was John Wesley, founder of Methodism. He was a strong abolitionist, famous for the sermons which he preached against "American slavery, the vilest that ever saw the sun." Many of the arguments which he used against the existence of slavery had been drawn from the works of the American Quaker, Anthony Benezet (1713 – 84), who also pioneered in such reform movements as women's education and fair treatment for Indians. Many of the abolitionists belonged to the manufacturing classes, or were successful merchants. Josiah Wedgwood, the famous potter, designed a medallion of a slave in chains, bearing the motto "Am I not a man and a brother?" It became the emblem of the Society for the Abolition of the Slave Trade and later of the American Anti-Slavery Society.

Members of the society, and fellow sympathizers, worked doggedly to erode the foundation of slavery upon which "King Sugar" rested.

They wrote books and pamphlets, describing to the British public the horrors of the Middle Passage — that is, the voyage of the slaves from Africa to America. They tried to combat the arguments put forward by their opponents that Britain's whole wealth rested on the slave trade and sugar, by pointing out that the slave trade, far from supporting the mercantile marine, caused a high death toll to British sailors, who often caught deadly fevers from the slaves.

Some abolitionists began the first food boycott in history, sweetening their coffee with cream instead of sugar, and asking for French brandy wherever they went, in place of rum. Others, and particularly the members of the Anti-Saccharite Society, told the public that "a family that uses 5 lbs. of sugar per week, will, by using East India instead of West India, for 21 months, prevent the slavery, or murder of one fellow-creature! Eight such families, in 19 and a half years, will prevent the slavery or murder of 100." To help abolotionists publicize their views, Mrs. B. Henderson, of the China Warehouse, Rye Lane, Peckham, London, sold sugar basins, handsomely labeled in gold letters: "East India sugar not made by slaves."

ABOLITION OF THE SLAVE TRADE

In 1722 the Society actually succeeded in getting some slaves freed, but only those whom their masters had brought to England. In 1807 the Whig Prime Minister of England, Charles James Fox, succeeded in banning the slave trade — so far as it applied to English ships. This meant that slavery in the English colonies would eventually die out, because the slave population in the Sugar Islands had to be constantly renewed by fresh importations. Then in 1833 slavery was finally abolished in the British Empire, the act becoming effective in 1834. The enormous sum — for the time — of £20 million was allotted to the slave owners as compensation, roughly £37 a slave. Unfortunately the sum was not fairly distributed. The West Indian plantation owners were ruined, and the Boer farmers at the Cape of Good Hope, embittered at the way the payments were made, began their Great Trek northward.

One factor which had held back the destruction of the sugar and slave trades had been the enormous fortunes made by everyone connected with sugar production — except, of course, the slaves. The people who profited most from sugar were the plantation owners, who either lived like princes in great mansions in the West Indies, or lorded it over English society in London. George III was astonished at the richness of a carriage owned by one of these West Indian nabobs, and remarked regretfully that he could never own one like it himself. In England the expression "as rich as a West Indian" was proverbial, and in 1803 the West Indies were responsible for one third of the imports and exports of Great Britain.

THE WEST INDIANS

The life of a rich West Indian planter (and they were all rich) just before the Age of Cane Sugar came to an end has been well painted for us by Lady Nugent, who accompanied her husband, Sir George Nugent, when he went out to be governor of Jamaica on April 1, 1801. The West Indies were as famous for their high death rate as for their wealth. "Nothing is ever talked of in this horrid island," writes Lady Nugent in her diary, "but the price of sugar. The only other topics of conversation are debt, disease, and death." Although the death rate of whites in the West Indies was bound to be high anyway, because they were living amidst tropical diseases, such as yellow fever, without having any of the immunities to those diseases that the Africans had, the planters decreased their chances of survival by the way they lived. It must be remembered that in those days with £30,000 a year they were much richer than an American millionaire nowadays.

Once they had built themselves splendid mansions with marble staircases and beautiful plaster ceilings, filled with Chippendale furniture, and bought every conceivable luxury in dress that could be imported from England, they spent a lot of money on eating and drinking.

I don't wonder, now [writes Lady Nugent] at the fever the people suffer from here — such eating and drinking I never saw! Such loads of rich and highly-seasoned things, and really the gallons of wine and mixed liquors that they drink. I observed some of our party today eat at breakfast as if they had never eaten before. A dish of tea, another of coffee, a bumper of claret, another large one of hock-negus; then Madeira, sangaree, hot and cold meats, stews and pies, hot and cold fish pickled and plain, peppers, ginger — sweetmeats, acid fruits, sweet jellies — in short it was all as astonishing as it was disgusting.

A little later she gives an account of a dinner.

The first course was of fish, with an entire jerked hog in the centre, and a black crab pepper-pot. The second course was of turtle, mutton, beef, turkey, goose, ducks, chicken, capons, ham, tongue, and crab patties. The third course was of sweets and fruits of all kinds. . . . I am not astonished,'' she adds, ''at the general ill-health of the men in this country, for they really eat like cormorants and drink like porpoises. All the men of our party got drunk tonight, even to a boy of fifteen, who was obliged to be carried home.

THE TRIANGLE OF TRADE

The Sugar Islands of the West Indies became one of the fixed points to and from which the trade of the whole British Empire flowed, in a system which was known as the Triangle of Trade. Ships would leave England loaded with trade goods for West Africa. There the goods would be converted into slaves. Special decks would now be fitted aboard the merchant ship, converting her into a slaver, large cauldrons for cooking food installed, and as much rice and water packed aboard the ship as she could hold. The slaves would then be manacled below decks, and the Middle Passage, or second leg of the triangle, would begin.

The slaver would hurry across the Atlantic, making what speed she could to avoid losing too many of the slaves. Not unfrequently disease would spread from below deck to the officers and crew, and it was not unknown for a slave ship to make port with everyone on board dead or dying. Once the slaver had cast anchor in a West Indian or American harbor, the slaves would be marched ashore and the extra decks knocked out. Loaded down with colonial produce such as sugar, rum, indigo, and tobacco, the ship would set out for England, to repeat the whole cycle again and again.

At various stages American traders joined in the beneficial economic effects of the Triangle of Trade. Newport, Rhode Island, was as famous a home port for the slavers as was Liverpool. They would sell American rum to the Africans for slaves. New England was famous for its distilleries, and there were sixty-three in Massachusetts alone in 1750. With the slaves they had obtained, they would trade in the West Indies, loading up with sugar and molasses for the American distilleries.

It was a great condescension on the part of the English government to allow Massachusetts to have any distilleries at all. Normally the economics of the British Empire was dominatd by what was called ''the old colonial system.'' England would produce all the manufactured goods, and would exchange them for the colonists' raw materials. This system worked better in some parts of the empire than others. The

British West Indians showed no desire to manufacture anything for themselves. They were content to grow sugar and exchange it for whatever they needed: sugar-refining cauldrons, cane-crushing machinery, machetes, cloth, luxuries, and so on. Every British West Indian was supposed to keep eight Englishmen continuously employed producing the goods he needed.

Yet while the West Indians were content, the Americans chafed at the restraints imposed on the newly developing American industries by England. They looked around for an opportunity to acquire economic independence — which of course could only be secured by achieving political independence as well. It was the rivalry between France and England for the Sugar Islands that gave them the needed opportunity.

IMPORTANCE OF THE SUGAR ISLANDS

The Sugar Islands were regarded by both Britain and France as their chief source of wealth in trade. France had fought hard to retain Canada during the eighteenth century, largely because she felt that Canada would be useful to exchange for one of her Sugar Islands if it were captured by England. Though the real wealth of England was beginning to change from sugar to the new industrial goods, produced by the infant Industrial Revolution, England was equally attached to the Sugar Islands, which she often regarded as the brightest jewel in her crown.

THE FIGHT FOR THE SUGAR ISLANDS

Both sides had captured each other's West Indian possessions during the eighteenth century, to retain them or hand them back as determined by the circumstances prevailing at the treaty negotiations. Then in 1761 the great British war minister William Pitt determined to end the struggle for sugar once and for all, in England's favor. The previous year British forces had seized St. Lucia and Guadeloupe. Now Pitt committed a great combined expedition of twelve ships of the line and twenty frigates together with a very considerable military force. Pitt was taking a gamble because the climate of the West Indies was deadlier to naval and military personnel than any opposing army.

It is ironic that the men who were expected to wrest France's Sugar Islands from her were not being fed any sugar themselves. The weekly ration for each soldier on West Indian service was four and a half pounds of bread, three fifths of a piece of beef and pork, one and a third pints of peas, a pint of oatmeal, a pint of "groats" (similar to "grits" eaten in the American South), half a pint of oil and a third of a pint of vinegar. The meat ration would work out at about six to twelve pounds weekly per man.

Pitt's gamble paid off, and Dominica, Martinique, Grenada, and St. Lucia were seized. Through the best two islands, Martinique and St. Lucia, were handed back to France at the Peace of Paris, the whole of the French *East* Indian Empire was simultaneously ceded to Britain, except for five trading posts. French sugar production had been dealt a very serious blow, and with it the prosperity of France as a whole.

The loss of the Sugar Islands to the French and their determination to get them back explains the otherwise inexplicable willingness of the French government to enter the War of American Independence on the side of the Americans. For France was tottering on the brink of bankruptcy. But the French ministers may well have felt that, if they could secure command of the sea and acquire bases in a victorious America, total control of the Caribbean was not too large an ambition to entertain.

Once Americans had proved their abilities in the field by forcing the surrender of General Burgoyne at Saratoga in 1777, the French leaped to sign a treaty of alliance with the shaky young republic. The French fleet under the Comte de Grasse sailed to the American coast, the Royal Navy, ineptly handled, lost control of the seas, and De Grasse's fleet was able to bottle up Cornwallis in Yorktown to await inevitable surrender.

Now De Grasse sailed southward to exact payment for France's help to the Americans by acquiring several, if not the whole of, British Sugar Islands.Off the Saints Islands, De Grasse sighted the English fleet under Admiral George Brydges Rodney from the deck of his flagship, the *Ville de Paris*. He jauntily announced to the French staff officers that in a very short time Rodney would be lunching aboard with them, a prisoner.

Instead, Rodney broke the French line in two places, and De Grasse found himself taking lunch with the English admiral aboard *his* flagship, the *Formidable*. There were to be no new sugar islands to help boost the staggering French economy.

Sailing past the scene of the battle during a holiday in 1871, Charles Kingsley, the Victorian naturalist and author, commented, "These islands were taken and retaken, till every gully held the skeleton of an Englishman. These seas were reddened with blood year after year, till the sharks learnt to gather to a sea fight as eagle, kite and wolf gathered of old to fights on land."

Even now, however, the sugar plant had not drunk its fill of human blood. The stay in Jamaica of Lady Nugent, mentioned earlier, was enlivened by the presence, on the nearby island of Haiti, of a dear friend called Madame Le Clerc Pauline. Le Clerc, later Princess Borghese, was the sister of Napoleon, and she had chosen to leave the frivolities of Paris and follow her husband, General le Clerc, to the deadliest climate in the world.

General Le Clerc had been sent to Haiti by Napoleon to try to put down the African rebellion there and recapture France's principal sugar island. It was a most ill-fated rebellion. Not only did the Africans resist stoutly (they had been declared free by the French Assembly in 1791 and had no intention of returning to slavery) but yellow fever took a terrible toll of the French. Altogether 40,000 Frenchmen, the flower of Napoleon's armies, died of fever, including Le Clerc. Pauline survived her husband and returned to France, where she was able to give her brother a personal account of the disaster.

Napoleon was well aware of the importance of sugar. He had himself married a girl from the plantation-owner class, Josephine Beauharnais. The Haiti disaster convinced him that it was hopeless to try to restore French authority in the Caribbean, but might it not be possible to produce sugar in France? If that could be done, then England's wealth, a by-product of cane sugar, would greatly suffer.

DISCOVERY OF BEET SUGAR

Other despots, notably Frederick the Great of Prussia, had toyed with the idea of starting colonial plantations at home, where exotic products could be grown without the need of colonies. Andreas Marggraff (1709 – 82) had published a paper on the extraction of sugar from sugar beet in 1744. His ideas were taken up and improved on by a French chemist, Benjamin Delessert, who began making beet sugar at Passy. So as to encourage sugar-beet production, the Emperor put 15,000 acres of land at the disposal of the French chemists who were carrying out the research, gave them a credit of a million francs, and promised them total exemption of taxes on all the sugar they produced for four years.

In 1812 Napoleon visited Delessert at his factory, and was so impressed by the sight of loaves of sugar, grown in France, that he divested himself of his own Cross of the Legion of Honor and pinned it on Delessert's breast.

In a speech a year or so previously, he had, as usual, anticipated success. "France will be able to dispense with the sugar and indigo of the East and West Indies. For the time being we can do without maritime commerce and colonies, until England returns to honorable and just principles, or until I can dictate terms of peace to her.

"Meanwhile, now that she can no longer sell her goods on the Continent, all the English can do is to throw into the Thames the sugar and indigo which they formerly sold, with such good profit to themselves, in Europe."

CONSEQUENCES OF SUGAR

The growth of a European sugar industry was only one of the factors which turned the West Indies from the most prosperous part of the Americas to the most economically depressed and backward. Liberty for the slaves — whether imposed by Act of Parliament or secured by Revolution, as in Haiti — did not bring the peace and prosperity for which the Evengelicals and Abolitionists had hoped. Yet it helped produce the first free black communities — the Republic of Haiti and smaller free black communities such as the Maroons of Accompong in Jamaica.

Sugar had altered the whole racial characteristic of the Caribbean. The Indians had been exterminated or driven away; the white communities, once thriving, had been dispersed by economic pressures, or massacred. A black diaspora had replaced the original inhabitants and their supplanters, and when the Africans had been freed from slavery and had decided to opt for subsistence farming rather than labor in the cane fields, new hands had been brought in from India and China, thus further altering the racial basis of the area.

Far afield the revolutionary influence of sugar made itself felt. Even in the distant Pacific a ship's crew, the complement of the *Bounty*, who had been engaged in transplanting the breadfruit tree from Tahiti to feed the slaves in the West Indies, mutinied and carried off their ship to Pitcairn Island, where their descendants, and those of the Tahitian girls they took with them, still remain. When at last the breadfruit tree did get established in the West Indies, the slaves refused to eat its fruit.

9.

The Agricultural Revolution

INCREASED FOOD PRODUCTION

During the Sugar Revolution millions had been enslaved, more millions slaughtered, and an even greater number forced to become the subjects of nations who lived on the other side of the globe from them. All this misery had been inflicted on Mankind simply to satisfy Western Europe's craving for something sweet. Yet sugar is not a necessity of life. It is merely a luxury food, like spices.

By contrast the next episode in the epic of food was to have much more beneficial results for the world as a whole. The Agricultural Revolution was going to double the food supply of the country in which it began during the lifetime of the founders of the revolution. By doing this, it would demonstrate to all the countries of the world that they might do the same. Yet it is noteworthy that the Agricultural Revolution originated from pretty much the same motives as those which inspired the slave trade — to make the participants rich. It just goes to show that there is nothing wrong with the profit motive, provided it can be harnessed to the right ends.

At the beginning of the eighteenth century, agriculture in England was in just about the same state that it had been during the Middle Ages, except that, through years of cultivation, the land was slightly less fertile.

All the cattle, except a very few, had to be killed as winter approached. The survivors, fed on chopped grass during the winter, were so thin and spindly that they often had to be carried out by their owners to crop the first spring pasture. At the best of times beef was tough, lean, and stringy; lamb was hard and bony, produced by animals kept more for wool than mutton. The yield from the fields was scanty, a thin crop mixed with weeds, some of them poisonous. Cultivation was half-hearted and careless; nobody bothered to improve his land by manuring it, because most English fields were shared out among the villagers as a whole. Every villager had a number of long strips in different fields, and these strips were redistributed from time to time.

English landowners were avid travelers. All of them, when they were young, tried to make the Grand Tour, a cultural trip through France and Switzerland to Italy. In between looking at ruins and pictures, the country squire who made the Grand Tour found time to wonder at the patient industry of the Italian vine dresser or the Dutch intensive farmer.

Would it not be possible, he must often have asked himself, to introduce intensive cultivation of this sort, not on the handkerchief-size fields of the Continent, but on the rolling acres of English farmland?

Words written by Jonathan Swift (1667 – 1745), the brilliant Irish satirist, about an imaginary island, in *Gulliver's Travels*, must have sunk home to the hearts of every Englishman:

> And he gave it for his opinion, that whoever could make two ears of corn, or two blades of grass, to grow where only one grew before, would deserve better of mankind, and do more essential service to his country, than the whole race of politicians put together.

It was not with the design of deserving better of mankind so much as in adding to their estates and rent rolls that the gentlemen of England now began to ponder changes in the growing of food crops. England was very well placed to undertake an Agricultural Revolution. The propertied classes tended to live in the country for a large part of the year, so if they invested in farming, they would be able to keep an eye on how their investment was progressing. In England, both law and custom gave people great freedom to do what they liked with their own property and also to introduce new ideas.

In France, for example, gentlemen were not expected to live on their own estates at all, but to attend the court at Versailles. A French nobleman could not engage in trade or he would have been degraded from his rank. In England a gentleman could marry into the merchant class and even engage in trade himself. Indeed, he was encouraged to enter the trade of brewing. Brewing used up much barley and hops, thus supporting other gentlemen, who made money out of farming.

In France, the animosities between different social classes were very great. This mistrust of his "betters" and obstinate conservatism were some of the reasons why it was almost impossible to introduce new farming ideas to the French peasant.

In England, on the other hand, the structure of society made it possible to put across new ideas in farming quite easily. The landowners controlled Parliament, so they were able to take the most important first step in the Agricultural Revolution — enclosure. The straggling strip cultivation of the English village disappeared. Instead of open fields, over which cattle roamed, breeding promiscuously and catching disease from one another, there appeared enclosed fields, fenced in with hedges. On these fields specialized livestock could be bred in seclusion, and special crops grown and intensively cultivated, without the weeds from one's neighbor's strip spoiling all the results of hard work.

ENCLOSURE

The Enclosure Movement did not take place without causing considerable hardship to the smallest landholders, and also the landless squatters who had only a cottage and a vegetable garden. These squatters had managed to eke out a living by pasturing a cow or perhaps a few geese on the village common pasture. A poet wrote:

> T'is very bad in man or woman,
> To steal a goose from off the common,
> But surely 'tis the worse abuse,
> To steal a common from the goose.

The squatters, and everyone else who could not make ends meet with the new farming, flocked to the industrial cities to hunt for work. They constituted the greatest incentive to the promoters of the Agricultural Revolution. They could not grow food for themselves in the cities, yet they had to be fed. Moreover the wages they got from industry were spent largely on food — and drink. So the new industrial masses constituted an enormous market for the increased production that the Agricultural Revolution was aimed at securing.

The hope of obtaining better and more plentiful food in the industrial cities was a strong lure for the displaced country people. In the country, village laborers ate very little, and most of that was bread. Occasionally, as a weekend treat, their wives might cook cabbage, with a tiny square of bacon on top. Otherwise their only relish with their eternal bread was cheese. As they only had a tiny piece of garden attached to their cottage, they could not keep a cow, and the farmer's butter, milk, and eggs were too dear for them to buy. If they were very lucky, they kept a pig, and its meat and by-products were the only animal food they saw from one year's end to another.

IMPROVED DIET IN TOWNS

Factory workers ate much better than those in the county. The city was the farmer's market, and as few farmers wished to transport back home unsold food, factory workers were able to bargain over prices. The factory worker's family could eat as much bread as they liked — say, twenty pounds a week. They also ate meat, five pounds a week. The town worker could treat himself to milk, butter, and eggs. Even if he were very short of money, he could feed himself a nourishing snack in the street, from a stall. This snack was often a few oysters, which before the "Whitstable Natives" of Britain had been destroyed by the slipper whelk (introduced with imported American spat), were incredibly cheap. "Oysters and poverty," wrote Charles Dickens in the following century, "go together."

BENJAMIN FRANKLIN IN LONDON

The industrial masses could afford to drink much more than their country counterparts. Young Ben Franklin, a visitor from America to London in 1724, has left us a graphic account of how much his fellow printers drank at the print room in Lincoln's Inn Fields.

> I drank only water, the other workmen, near fifty in number, were great drinkers of beer. On occasion, I carried up and down stairs a large form* of type in each hand, when others carried up but one in both hands. They wondered to see, from this and several other instances, that the *Water*

*A wooden frame containing a page of type, locked in place with quoins and other type "furniture."

American, as they called me, was *stronger* than themselves, who drank strong beer!

We had an alehouse boy who attended always in the house to supply the workmen. My companion at the press drank every day a pint before breakfast, a pint at breakfast with his bread and cheese, a pint between breakfast and dinner, a pint at dinner, a pint in the afternoon about six o'clock, and another when he had done his day's work.

I thought it a detestable custom; but it was, he supposed, to drink *strong beer,* that he might be strong to labor. I endeavored to convince him that the bodily strength afforded by beer could only be in proportion to the grain or flour of the barley dissolved in the water of which it was made; that there was more flour in a pennyworth of bread, and therefore if he could eat that with a pint of water, it would give him more strength than a quart of beer.

He drank on, however, and had four or five shillings* to pay out of his wages every Saturday night for that vile liquor; an expense I was free from. And thus these poor devils keep themselves always under. . . .

The printers drank so much on Sunday, their only holiday, that on Monday they rarely came in to work at all. So as a joke, Monday was often referred to as "St. Monday" as if it were a public holiday. "I, never making a St. Monday, writes Franklin, recommended me to my master." Because he never drank, he was promoted to working at a higher branch of the craft. What happened then is an illustration of the enormous social pressure exerted on people to make them drink, whether they want to or not.

> When Franklin arrived in the composing room, the compositors demanded that he should pay them five shillings for drink, because he was a new arrival. He objected to this as he had paid the pressmen drinking money when he joined the firm, only a few weeks before. "I stood out two or three weeks," he says in his *Autobiography,* "and was accordingly considered as an excommunicate and had so many little pieces of private malice practised on me, by mixing up my type, etc., if ever I stepped out of the room, and all ascribed to the *chapel ghost,* which they said ever haunted those not regularly admitted, that . . . I found myself obliged to comply and pay the money."

---

*Which meant that, at three halfpence for a pint, the workman had drunk forty pints in the working week, Monday to Saturday. "From my example, "adds Franklin," a great many of them left their muddling breakfast of beer, bread and cheese, finding they could, with me, be supplied from a neighbouring house with a large porringer of hot water-gruel, sprinkled with pepper, crumbed with bread, and a bit of butter in it, for the price of a pint of beer, viz. three halfpence. This was a more comfortable as well as a cheaper breakfast and kept their heads clearer."

FARMING INVENTIONS

In order to realize the profits to be made from this enormous home market of industrial eaters and drinkers, the shrewd English landowners now attempted a several-pronged attack on the problem of increasing food production.

One way has already been noticed — enclosing the old common fields and cottagers' strips and replacing them with fenced enclosures. Another was developing new systems of cultivation. Jethro Tull, an Oxford law student who had been forced to abandon the law because of bad health and became a farmer instead, led this particular movement. Instead of simply throwing seed corn out of a basket onto the land, he drilled every piece of seed into the ground and howed between the rows of growing corn with a horse hoe.

Viscount Townshend, a statesman who had left politics after a quarrel with his brother-in-law, Prime Minister, Robert Walpole, started growing new vegetables, such as clover and turnips. The turnips made it possible to keep cattle right through the winter by feeding them on root crops. This in turn meant that it was now possible to ensure supplies of milk and butter the year round. Townshend also started growing continuous crops on the different fields of his farm, instead of just letting part of it lie fallow, which had been the practice hitherto.

Perhaps the most impressive change in farming during this period was the work of Robert Bakewell. Bakewell began to do with cattle and sheep what the owners of racehorses and riding studs had been doing for decades. He selected the best breeding stock, and ensured that their descendants bred with none other than prime farm stock.

The results of his experiments, and those of the Collings brothers, were very striking. The average weight of beeves at Smithfield Market in London rose from 370 pounds in 1710 to 800 in 1795. Calves went up from 50 pounds to 148 pounds, and sheep from 28 pounds to 80 pounds.

Soon model farming was all the rage. George III set up a model farm at Windsor and introduced a stock of the new Merino sheep. Overseas, Thomas Jefferson turned Monticello into a miniature agricultural experiment station, trying out plants and animals from all over the world. Gentlemen with botanical interests corresponded far and wide and exchanged plant specimens for experiment wherever there was a suitable garden or farm plot.

The Agricultural Revolution had more important results than anything that had happened in the history of farming since the Neolithic

Farming Revolution. Food production was enormously increased, and the food produced was much more wholesome than when meat had been obtained from spindly diseased cattle and bread from blighted wheat. Gone were the hard times of winter, when in the past there had been no meat, no butter, no milk, and no vegetables — nothing but hoarded stores. The effect of this change on the diet of the English population as a whole was striking. Infants, who could now get continuous supplies of milk, were much more likely to survive early childhood. Adults, fed on a diet containing more protein and vitamins, tended to produce more and healthier children, who would live to grow up and have children of their own.

POPULATION EXPLOSION

The first important population stemmed from the Agrarian Revolution in England. Thomas Malthus (1766 – 1834), an English economist who was a contemporary of this revolution, was the first to point out that the arrival of scientific agriculture had not solved all mankind's problems, only increased them. While food production increased in an arithmetical progression (where the increase is measured by addition), population increased in a geometrical progression (where the increase is measured by multiplication). His worst predictions seemed to have been realized in 1792 when there was a surplus of English wheat for export for the last time. Thereafter, Britain was to be increasingly reminded that she was an island. If anything happened to stop imports of food from abroad, her population would simply starve to death.

REVOLUTION IN AMERICA

In the meantime, the Agricultural Revolution had moved overseas. As soon as the ideas of the founders of farming reform got into print, they were being read on the other side of the Atlantic. American pilgrims arrived at the sheep-shearing festival which Thomas Coke of Holkam (1752 – 1842) held every year on his estate. There they would hear about the new farming methods which were being evolved so rapidly in England and be able to put them into effect on their own land in America.

But it was not until the tide of settlement had crossed the mountain barrier and was spreading through the fertile Midwest, across the Mississippi and out onto the vast prairies, that new methods of farming began to change the face of America. New methods were needed. The tough-rooted grasslands resisted the feeble iron plows the settlers had brought with them, and the back-breaking labor of harvesting limited the amount a man could plant and reap from his new soil. Wheat was particularly frustrating. There were only about ten days in which to harvest the delicate grains before they were lost, and a man with a scythe could cut only half an acre a day. That limited plantings to five acres for every able-bodied man on the farm — scarcely enough to feed him and his family.

But American farmers, long beset by a shortage of labor, were confirmed tinkerers, skilled at rigging up devices to perform such tedious chores as apple peeling and log barking, and they began to turn these inventive skills toward the development of farm machinery. In 1831, a young Virginia blacksmith named Cyrus Hall McCormick demonstrated the first practical mechanical reaper. In one day it reaped seven full acres of oats and could easily perform the same function for wheat, barley, or rye. By 1844, McCormick had perfected a model that could reap sixteen acres a day and was selling them at the rate of two hundred a year. Indeed, in an emergency — illness of the husband, a war, widowhood — the mechanical reaper enabled women to do the work of men.

In 1837, meanwhile, John Deere had patented his steel plow, capable of cutting through the matted root system of the prairie sod and turning it back like a blanket, opening the virgin soil to the planting. The cultivator, the disk harrow, mowing devices, the mechanical thresher worked by steam, and that ultimate tamer of the open range, barbed wire, all followed. Mail-order companies like Sears, Roebuck and Montgomery Ward were founded to enable isolated farm wives to shop from a catalog. Mishawaka, Indiana, grew prosperous constructing windmills to pump water for the prairie farmer. The Midwest was soon golden with grain.

In 1861, a mere thirty years after McCormick first demonstrated his invention, novelist Anthony Trollope visited Canada and the United States and described the results of this blossoming:

> I was at Chicago and at Buffalo in October 1861. I went down to the granaries and climbed up into the elevators. I saw the wheat running in rivers from one vessel into another, and from the railroad vans up into the huge bins on the top stories of the warehouses; — for these rivers of food

run up hill as easily as they do down. I saw the corn measured by the forty bushel measure with as much ease as we measure an ounce of cheese, and with greater rapidity. I ascertained that the work went on, week day and Sunday, day and night incessantly; rivers of wheat and rivers of maize ever running. I saw the men bathed in corn as they distributed it in its flow. I saw bins by the score laden with wheat, in each of which bins there was space for a comfortable residence. I breathed the flour, and drank the flour, and felt myself to be enveloped in a world of breadstuff. And then I believed, understood, and brought it home to myself as a fact, that here in the corn lands of Michigan, and amidst the bluffs of Wisconsin, and on the high table plains of Minnesota, and the prairies of Illinois, had God prepared the food for the increasing millions of the Eastern world, as for the coming millions of the Western.

Even while Trollope was writing that, his country was debating what to do about the American Civil War, then raging. The Federal blockade of Southern ports, which prevented cotton from being shipped abroad to English cotton mills, had caused severe hardship among the starving millhands, and a certain element of the British public favored a bold attempt to break the blockade and carry off the cotton by main force. After all, the French under Louis Napoleon had taken advantage of American preoccupation to invade Mexico and establish an ''empire'' with a Hapsburg at its head Why not a much milder action on the part of the English?

But while Victoria's government hesitated, food settled the question. For the island kingdom suddenly discovered that, much as it needed Southern cotton, it needed Northern wheat even more. The English kept hands off — and turned to other sources for cotton.

And in the fullness of time, Trollope's prediction came true, for today the New World has become in large measure the granary of the Old — Argentina, Canada, Australia, and the United States among them supplying grain to nearly the whole of Europe and European Russia.

10.

The Preserving Of Food

The art of preserving food successfully had its start — as have so many things — in a war effort. In an attempt to isolate his enemy Great Britain, Napoleon Bonaparte in 1806 declared the island kingdom under blockade. He issued a series of decrees from his newly captured capital of Prussia, Berlin, that the whole of the British Isles was closed to shipping from the French Empire and those countries allied to her — virtually the whole of Europe.

THE CONTINENTAL SYSTEM BACKFIRES

But this was a paper blockade, ineffectual without a navy to back it up, and it was Great Britain which had the navy. One by one, the satellite states began to break the rules he had laid down about not trading with England. Countries like Holland (where he had to depose his own brother because of breaches of the Continental System), Sweden, Russia, and Portugal were avid to obtain the goods that only England had to sell, particularly colonial products such as coffee and sugar. Those countries which were too loyal to Napoleon to break his regulations, and they were not many, writhed under a sense of deprivation. The Danes had become a nation of coffee drinkers,* yet there was not a cup of coffee to be had in all Denmark. The ersatz coffee made from acorns and barley, which Napoleon had suggested that his subjects drink instead, tasted so unpleasant that no one would drink it. (Napoleon himself drank innumerable cups of real coffee, which had come from Mocha in Arabia and which he had bought directly from England — because he was prepared to break his own rules.) A hundredweight of coffee was quoted at $10,000 (in modern equivalents) on the Hamburg Stock Exchange, and this was merely a notional price, for there was none available (except in the Tuileries Palace).

Breaches of the Continental System became more and more flagrant, particularly in Portugal where chocolate played the same part that coffee did in Denmark. So Napoleon marched into Portugal to teach its inhabitants a lesson, overthrowing the Spanish royal family and replacing them with one of his brothers on the way.

FOOD AS A WEAPON

Now, the name of Portugal was on every well-to-do Englishman's lips, for when dinner was finished and the ladies had retired, port — a strong, fruity wine from Oporto in Portugal — was brought to every gentleman's table. England had had trading ties with Portugal since the fourteenth century, and by a curious coincidence her other great wine, sherry, came from Xeres, in Spain, the other country which Napoleon had now outraged. To checkmate her great enemy, and to secure the two commodities essential for every gentleman's dinner, England dispatched an expeditionary force to Portugal under Sir Arthur Wellesley.

Wellesley had a sharp eye for the weaknesses of his opponents. Now Napoleon's greatest weakness was that, instead of issuing rations to his troops, he simply ordered them to feed themselves off the countryside. This system had always worked well hitherto. The inhabitants of the lands into which the French armies marched had hastened to place all their food supplies at the disposal of the soldiers, even if it meant starving themselves, for there are worse fates than starvation.

But Portugal, and for that matter the whole of the Iberian peninsula, was a different terrain from that in which the Napoleonic armies had

*A King of Denmark had once imprisoned twin murderers for life, ordering that one was to drink nothing but coffee, the other nothing but tea. When the tea-drinking twin died at the age of eighty, the Danes decided that the controversy which had raged about the relative merits of the two drinks had now been settled in favor of coffee.

campaigned hitherto. Parts of Spain and Portugal were a virtual desert.

Wellington now decided to put the sterile nature of the Iberian countryside to work for him. He ordered a series of fortifications built across the neck of the peninsula on which Lisbon stands. These "Lines of Torres Vedras" became an impregnable fortress into which the British and their Portuguese allies could retire, sweeping up with them all the food available. The French, under one of Napoleon's best marshals, Soult, wore themselves out with months of fruitless attacks in 1811. Then, having exhausted all their supplies, they were forced by starvation to retreat.

NAPOLEON'S OWN EATING HABITS

Napoleon did not profit from this lesson. Instead of putting the French army commissariat on a proper footing, and spending some of the millions he had looted from Europe on feeding his men, he went on as before. In theory, nobody was better aware of the need for a commissariat than Napoleon. He is the author of the famous dictum, "An army marches on its stomach," and he himself maintained a beautifully appointed camp kitchen, which followed him about everywhere, to supply meals for himself and a few cronies.

Napoleon himself was one of history's most erratic eaters. He had inherited chronic dyspepsia from his father — "My only inheritance," he once remarked bitterly — and he was a compulsive gobbler. He took twelve minutes to eat a meal if there were company present, eight if he were eating alone. Dinner times meant nothing to him. Four hours after he was due to sit down to table, he would still be reviewing his troops. It was not unusual for him to work eighteen hours at a stretch, taking nothing but a cup of coffee as nourishment. Then suddenly he would remember that he had not eaten, and would cry to his faithful valet, "Constant, my dinner this instant." Like all his other orders, this had to be obeyed on the dot.

Napoleon's kitchen staff made a gallant attempt to accommodate themselves to the great man's demands. Borel, the second cook, put on a chicken to roast an hour or so before dinner time. Another followed some twenty minutes later, then a third, and so on, until Napoleon finally called for dinner. Then the chicken of the minute would be served up, straight from the spit.

THE INVASION OF RUSSIA

Just a year after Torres Vedras Napoleon repeated the same blunder he had made in Spain. He led the largest army ever assembled, 610,000 men, across the River Niemen into Russia. Russia had offended him by refusing to put the Continental System into practice. The soldiers of the *Grande Armée* only had three weeks' rations in their haversacks. Unless they won a battle during that period of time they would have to feed themselves from the Russian countryside — or starve.

Their leader might well have argued that, after all, Russia was not a desert, like Spain. It was the breadbasket of Europe, the country which had the biggest surplus of grain for export. It was harvest time, and in any case the Czar would soon surrender. All Napoleon's assumptions proved to be incorrect. The Czar did not surrender; instead he ordered that all the food in the path of the advancing French armies should be destroyed.

Napoleon's repetition of a former mistake was undoubtedly due to the fact that his judgment was failing. His aide-de-camp, Comte Philippe de Ségur, paints a dreadful picture of how his chief mismanaged the greatest military adventure in history, gazing out on the world with lackluster eyes, giving orders about forces which did not exist, unable either to listen to advice or issue the directives necessary to save his army.

The French, and their Italian, Polish, and German allies retreated through the snow back toward Poland, too happy when they were able to find the frozen carcasses of dead horses to eat. A certain Sergeant Bourgogne was once lucky enough to find three frozen potatoes. He hurried off into the darkness away from the campfire, meaning to keep them all to himself. But as his teeth grated on the frozen potatoes he felt the tears trickling down his cheeks at his disloyalty in betraying his comrades in this way, so he made his way back into the firelight and threw the potatoes into the communal camp kettle around which his companions were sitting.

If Napoleon had taken advantage of a newly discovered method of preserving food for an indefinite period — for which he himself had handed out an award of 12,000 francs — the outcome of the Russian campaign might have been different. Napoleon had been very eager to promote the discovery of practical ways of putting up food.

One method was that of Sir Benjamin Thompson, Count Rumford

(1753–1814), an American-born physicist and inventor. While in service to the Duke of Bavaria, Rumford invented packet food — his famous "portable soup." Made from a solidified stock of veal, meat trimmings, or pork offcuts, plus other nourishing ingredients, it was a kind of bouillon cube which was used by soup kitchens to make a cheap but nutritious soup to feed the poor.

But this was too limited a technique. The real problem was to find ways to preserve solid food. It was well known that the more air excluded from a food product, the longer it was likely to last. Giovanni Casanova (1725–98), the famous Venetian traveler, had bought pies and patés which could be dispatched right across Europe and arrive in as good condition as when they were baked. Presumably the pastry cook had enclosed them in an airtight casing of wax, as many cheeses are packaged today. The Italian naturalist Lazzaro Spallanzani (1729–99) had demonstrated that organic substances boiled in enclosed vessels do not decay; it is contact with the air that causes putrefaction. Experiments in France had proved that meat, cut into small morsels, would keep for quite a time when tightly corked in a champagne bottle.

Nicolas Appert (1749–1841) carried all this a logical step further. Established as a confectioner in Paris before the French Revolution, he began experimenting with various methods. Eventually he settled on a technique of placing food in glass bottles, which were then heated in an open water bath — what the French call a *bain marie*. The length of cooking time varied with the type of food under treatment. While they were still boiling, the bottles, wide-necked, were corked with waxed corks, and these were later wired in place like the corks of modern champagne bottles.

Appert's discovery had its good points and bad. The glass bottles and wax corks were completely free of contamination, and they would not rust or decay. But the glass was very easy to break or crack, and any opening, even a hair-line fracture, could admit enough air to contaminate the entire contents of the bottle unperceived.

However, when Napoleon heard of this discovery, he gave Appert the money award with the stipulation that he publish information about it. Accordingly, in 1810 Appert published a work entitled *A Book for All Housekeepers* or *The Art of Preserving All Kinds of Animal and Vegetable Substances for Several Years*. It was the basis for all subsequent advances in home and commercial canning, drying, and freezing of foodstuffs.

THE FIRST TIN CANS

The next step in the food-preservation story was taken by an English inventor, Bryan Donkin (1768 – 1855). Donkin's early o ork was chiefly in the papermaking and printing fields, but living as he did during the Napoleonic Wars, it was natural that he should be interested in military commissariat. Since he held shares in an ironwork, it was also natural that he should substitute tinplate for Appert's glass containers. The new canisters were hand-formed tin cans, made at first with a little hole in the top through which they were filled. While the contents were boiling, a cap was soldered over this hole. The containers were virtually unbreakable.

By 1812 Donkin had abandoned his other projects to concentrate on his new process. He set up a factory to make cans — or tins, as they are still called in England — and by 1818 his boiled beef, corned beef, mutton, vegetable stew, and soup had begun to reach a rich and exclusive clientele.

Donkin was shrewd enough to realize that, if canned food was ever to find its way into the soldier's ration, it would have to start in the officers' mess. He went straight to the top of the army list and approached the commander in chief of the British Army, Frederick Augustus, Duke of York, who was George III's second son. "The Grand Old Duke of York" approved of Donkin's "patent beef," and orders were placed for the Royal Family and the Royal Navy. "Salt horse" was on its way out.

THE EFFECTS OF CANNING

The invention of the tinned can made life much healthier aboard ships. It was now possible to serve not only meat which was not absolutely stinking but ship's biscuit that was free of weevils. The combination of tin cans and machine-baked biscuit meant that the seaman's bread could be hermetically sealed within an hour or so of baking. The flour, ground by a steam mill, was mixed by machinery, kneaded by enormous iron cylinders, and sliced into large sheets of almost complete biscuits, which baked in twelve minutes. The finished product, broken from the large sheet, could then be stored in sealed tin cans. The weevil had no chance to get at them and lay its eggs, and so the biscuit weevil disappeared from maritime history.

The virtues of tinplate were next applied to ship's drinking water. In wooden barrels, water soon became a green, scummy liquid and in tropical seas was an open invitation to the yellow-fever mosquito, which laid its eggs in stagnant water.* Kept in tinned tanks, later in galvanized-iron tanks, it remained fresh the whole voyage.

Food continued to be dreary, monotonous, and badly cooked, however, in the world's biggest mercantile fleet, that of Great Britain. While French whalers carried dried and fresh vegetables, coffee from Haiti, American sausages, English ham and bacon, dried Icelandic codfish, rice from Rangoon, gin from Holland, olive oil from Nice, black and green tea from China, and live pigs, hens, ducks, and geese from Brittany, the menu aboard an English ship continued to be well-nigh uneatable. It is small wonder that, in the years before 1812, British seamen deserted to the American navy in droves; the work was just as hard, the discipline just as brutal, but the food was incomparably better, and there was much more of it — two and a half times the ration aboard a British ship.

A century later the situation had not improved much, and one consequence was that few British seamen would serve in British merchant ships. They were manned almost exclusively by Germans and Scandinavians. It was even suggested, on the eve of World War I, that Germany could easily seize control of the British mercantile marine by simple mutiny.

THE PRESERVATION OF MILK

Canning meanwhile had crossed the Atlantic, where canneries were established chiefly along the ocean, putting up oysters, fish, and lobster in cold weather, and corn, tomatoes, and peas in the summer. But one food product eluded canners. Milk could be preserved in cans but not in potable form.

Then in 1851 a Texas inventor named Gail Borden, who had attended the Great Exhibition at the Crystal Palace to show off a dried meat "biscuit" he had developed, found himself enduring a rough sea voyage home. Nobody was comfortable, but the worst sufferers were the young children of immigrant families. The cows, brought along to supply fresh milk during the voyage, were too seasick to be milked. Borden set about finding a way to condense and can whole milk.

---

* One of the great mysteries of maritime hygiene was that, although illness and death from communicable disease normally diminished the longer a ship was at sea, yellow fever was the great exception. An outbreak could appear many weeks after the ship had cleared its last port. Later, of course, men learned that the insect laid its eggs in the open casks of water — to hatch while the vessel was in mid-ocean.

After several abortive attempts he hit on a method that worked — evaporating it in a vacuum pan. In 1856 the process was patented and came on the market just in time for the American Civil War. The Federal government bought up his entire output. Borden's standards of hygiene were high, and until Pasteur's work demonstrated the technique of pasteurization, it was the safest and most digestible milk available.

Yet the tinplate revolution was not without its drawbacks. It introduced another unwanted food additive to the human diet, dissolved salts of tin. But a lacquer lining in cans soon helped to end the solvent effect.

A much more serious drawback to tinned foods was that it made life easier for the militarist. American soldiers, fed largely on canned pork and beans, invented their own words to the tune of mess call: "Come and get your beans, boys, come and get your beans." By 1850 "bully beef" (from *boeuf bouillie,* "boiled beef"), or canned cornbeef from Argentina, was synonymous with life in the British army or navy and later as much a part of World War I as the machine gun and barbed wire. (German soldiers were unaccountably fond of English bully beef and always carried off armfuls of it during raids.) In World War II, although Britain was woefully short of agricultural land, fields were set aside to grow gherkins and onions; these vegetables give little nourishment, but no British soldier would dream of eating tinned meat without pickles.

On balance, though, the canning revolution was a great advance. Cowboys on Western rangelands could eat peaches in midwinter. Canned tomatoes supplied vitamin C to diets that were deficient of it. Canned lamb from sunny countries like Argentina, Australia, and New Zealand dealt a blow to that dreadful children's disease, rickets — a godsend to dwellers in cloudy northern Europe.

From Nicolas Appert's first invention stemmed the techniques so run-of-the-mill today: refrigeration, which brought fresh meat to the table year-round; the Mason jar, which made home-canning possible; frozen foods, freeze-dried foods, mixes, fresh dairy products, packaged baked goods. Gail Borden, a firm believer in finding new ways to store food, once said, "The Turks made acres of roses into attar of roses. . . . I intend to make attar of everything." He died before he succeeded, but his descendants have seen it come to pass.

11.

The Transport Revolution

FOOD AND TRANSPORT

There was a striking connection between famine and transport — or rather lack of transport. The unknown Pharaoh who commissioned Joseph to institute the biggest antifamine project in the Bible evidently did not envisage any problems about distributing the surplus grain that was to be stored during the "seven fat years." The Nile would provide a transport highway for people to get to the royal granaries.

Other countries were not so fortunate. China, where there had been a famine every second year since history began, was a case in point. If a grain surplus existed anywhere in the Chinese Empire, it was almost impossible to get it to the scene of the famine. An official report quoted by American writer W.H. Mallory paints a fearful picture of the famine of 1876 – 1879.

During the winter and spring of 1877 – 78, the most frightful disorder reigned supreme along the route to Shansi. Fugitives, beggars, and thieves absolutely swarmed. The officials were powerless to create any sort of order among the mountains. The track was completely worn out. Camels, oxen, mules, and donkeys were hurried along in the wildest confusion. . . . Night travelling was out of the question. The way was marked by the carcasses of men and beasts, and the wolves, dogs, and foxes soon put an end to the sufferings of any wretch who lay down to recover from or die of his sickness. Broken carts, scattered grain bags, dying men and animals so frequently stopped the way, that it was often necessary to prevent for days together the entry of convoys on the one side, in order to let the trains from the other come over.

Yet paradoxically enough, while one part of a country might be suffering from famine, another might be enjoying relative plenty. Consider the case of two villages we happen to know about because they have been the subject of close study by population historians. In 1645 the villagers of Colyton, Devonshire, England, were starving to death. In that same year, fifty miles to the west, those of Hartland had had an excellent harvest. If a canal, or any other efficient form of transport, had existed between the two villages, then the inhabitants of Colyton might have been able to buy their neighbors' surplus.

It was to make a profit — by selling a commodity which was surplus in one area in another area where it was in short supply — that the Transport Revolution came into being. The vehicles which were to make it possible were the canal barge, the fast-sailing clipper ship, the steamboat, and the locomotive. All these devices were to have an enormous effect not just in abating the horrors of famine, but in shaping the America we know today.

TRANSPORT INVENTIONS

Of these transport inventions, two were purely by American, the clipper ship and the steamboat, while another, the railroad locomotive, was created by George Stephenson of Great Britain.

All these vehicles contributed, in a greater or less degree, to the Transport Revolution. They brought down the price of food, by removing food surpluses from the farms to the cities, by widening the market, and by increasing production. In the past, unsold cabbages had remained with the farmer. Now they were shuttled to the big cities by railroad or canal. If they could not be sold fresh at full price, then they were sold much more cheaply a day or so later. In the open markets where most city produce was sold, the prices of food tended to drop toward the end of the day. By shopping just before the market closed, you could buy more for less. So, for the first time the poor were able to bargain for cheaper food. Farmers themselves were encouraged to enter the produce market, who had previously confined themselves to growing cereals or other bulk food that did not require rapid transit.

Much of the milk for big cities like London had been obtained from cows kept in city cellars, knee-deep in filth. In New York, cows were fed distillery swill, and since the distilling process had drawn off much of the nourishment from the grain, this "swill milk" was of little nutritive value. The advent of the steam locomotive now meant that fresh milk could be hauled to the cities from a considerable distance, sometimes more than a hundred miles away. In England, it was brought by what was traditionally the first train of the day, the milk train.

FRESH FISH AND POULTRY

The speed of food transport meant that food was now a lot fresher than before and consequently much richer in vitamins. In the past the only way to get fresh poultry to the big cities was to drive the birds there alive, in great flocks. In the Orkney Islands, north of Scotland, geese would be rounded up, driven through a bath of melted pitch and then across piles of sand. This would give the birds a stout pair of boots to protect their feet for the long march south. They would then be ferried to mainland Scotland and herded mile by mile all the way to the poultry markets of London, stopping for a feed and a rest several times a day. Fresh geese, driven to market this way, were, of course, expensive and usually ended up on the tables of the rich.

As for marine fish, there was no way of getting it to market in edible condition — except for oysters brought in barrels of brine.

But with the advent of the railroad, all that changed. Poultry could be raised almost anywhere in England and carried to market live or fresh-killed. Instead of arriving at the markets having lost much of their weight and food value from their long journey, they would taste just like "a pullet off the midden" — that is, straight from the farmyard. Fish was brought at full speed from the fishing grounds, having been caught by the new steam trawlers and brought back to port by a special transport ship, then shipped to the city packed in ice.

Ice for preservation had been known since Roman times. It was natural ice, cut from rivers and lakes during the winter, and kept in domed ice houses under straw during the summer. (By 1821, Frederic Tudor, an enterprising Bostonian, had learned to preserve ice so well that he was shipping cargoes of it to India.) But now in combination with fast vessels and trains, it enabled cargoes of fresh fish to be carried to the far interiors of such countries as France, where marine fish had been unknown before. Its presence in the diet helped combat a disease which had once scourged areas far from the sea — goiter, caused by an insufficiency of iodine.

The new techniques also made possible the familiar food of the British poor, fish and chips. Though the origin of this combination has always eluded food historians, I believe that the fried fish originated in the large colonies of Jewish refugees from Russia and Poland who began to settle in London, Leeds, and other large towns in the midnineteenth century. On their arrival, people commented on the smell of frying fish, which was characteristic of their neighborhoods. Shortly afterward, the whole of England smelled of frying fish.

AMERICAN RAILROADS

Hard times in Europe, and notably in Ireland, had brought many new citizens to the expanding United States; many flocked out to the opening West. It was American policy to encourage westward settlement. Government and state land was sold very cheaply to settlers or given away to homesteaders who would settle on a quarter section (160 acres), build a house, and farm it for five years. To such farm owners, the new American railroads now offered all kinds of concessions. The Western farmer was offered a freight reduction known as "a long haul for the price of a short haul." The railroad companies even advertised for settlers in Europe and sold them great blocks of land they had acquired as the government's way of encouraging their growth.

It was not just the prairie farmer, growing bumper crops on virgin soil, who benefited from the new railroads. Workmen and the public did also. The Union Pacific line was laid by Irish immigrants working from the east across the prairies and by Chinese immigrants working from the west through the Sierras. Snow sheds miles long protected the cars from disastrous blizzards like those which had marooned the Donner party in the mountains in 1847.

Many American towns owed their existence to the railroad. One such was Abilene, Kansas, northern terminus of the famed Chisholm trail. To its stockyards cowboys drove 700,000 longhorn cattle a year along the 700-mile route from San Antonio. From Abilene the cattle traveled down the line to the meat-packing plants of Chicago and Kansas City. But it was the coming of the refrigerated cars that created the great packing industry.

Two Chicagoans, Philip Armour and Gustavus Swift, rival entrepreneurs, conceived roughly the same idea — that meat would come to market cheaper and in better condition if shipped off the hoof, saving space and shipping costs on those parts that could not be sold. (There weren't many.) That meant using refrigerated cars and setting up elaborate arrangements for maintaining the low temperatures that protected the sides of beef from spoiling. Railroads did not want the refrigerated cars, preferring the higher rates for shipping live cattle, but the two men designed their own cars and within ten years were routinely delivering Chicago-slaughtered meat to East Coast butchers.

A nineteenth-century visitor to a pork-packing company described it thus:

> The slaughtering and packing establishments at Chicago are on an extensive and very complete scale and worked by steam. With incredible rapidity the animal is lifted, killed, washed, scraped, brushed, gutted, cleaned, and dismembered. Each part salted or smoked is then put into boxes or barrels, and is ready to be sent into commerce. From 1,000 to 2,000 pigs can thus be dispatched daily in single establishments.

Meat packing was highly profitable. Eventually every part of the hog was put to use — except, as one Chicagoan remarked, the curl in the animal's tail. At first, hams and sides alone were used. Soon heads, feet, trotters, and cheeks went into the sausage vats. The bristles were removed and made into brushes, the fine hair washed, dried, cured, and used for stuffing mattresses. The hide became pigskin gloves. The oil was squeezed out of the lard with machinery, then what remained was made into stearine candles. Lastly, the blood was turned into prussiate of potash (potassium cyanide).

WATER TRANSPORT

While the railroads steamed on, other transport inventions had not stood still either. The fast canal boats which traveled the Erie Canal, completed in 1825, linking Albany on the Hudson with Buffalo on Lake Erie, carried farming immigrants westward and returned laden with the fruits of their toil. The "river of grain" Trollope saw in 1861 was shipped through the Great Lakes and across New York State by barge to the transatlantic ships, waiting to load wheat and corn.

The steamboat, the glory of American rivers and still remembered romantically in novels and movies, was first used to haul lines of canal barges down the Hudson to New York City. Steamboats also hauled milk prosaically between the Erie Railroad's terminus at Piermont down the Hudson to the city. But steamboats were associated more with carrying cotton downriver and passengers up river, than with hauling foodstuffs.

Not so with another American invention, the swift sailing vessel known as the clipper ship. The clipper's best-known service was in the tea trade between London and Canton, China's great tea port.

The first real clipper ship, *Ann McKim,* was built in Baltimore in 1833. She owed a good deal to the topsail schooners called Baltimore clippers that had been built in Chesapeake Bay since the 1750's, and her lines were unlike any square-rigged ship ever launched. She had a sharp, narrow bow, which cut the water like a razor, narrow moldings, fine lines, and a great spread of canvas aloft. She and her sister ships set the style for American shipbuilders for decades, producing such immortals as the *Flying Cloud* (eighty-nine days from New York to San Francisco around the Horn, a record under sail that still stands), the *Sea Witch* (seventy-four days, fourteen hours, Canton to New York), *Champion of the Seas* (465 nautical miles logged in one day), and others.

Many of these vessels were sailing around the Horn because gold had been discovered in California, and Europeans and Easterners were clamoring to get to the goldfields. Having delivered their human cargo at San Francisco, the emigrant ships would have had to return home in ballast. Instead, most preferred to pick up a cargo and sail directly for Europe. The natural choice was tea — light cargo, easily stowed, and available in great quantities at Canton.

There was another excellent reason for choosing tea. The English were avid tea drinkers, and they had only recently opened their ports (where foreign bottoms had hitherto suffered under certain restrictions) to free trade. Here, the fast-sailing qualities of the clipper were of great advantage, because the tea drinkers of Great Britain preferred "new tea" — that is, this year's crop.

The first American tea clipper to arrive in London was the *Oriental,* which came into the West India Docks in 1850, having made a record passage out from Canton in only ninety-seven days, though it was the wrong time of the year to set up sailing records. Everyone was amazed at her lines, longer and narrower than anything seen in a British dock before. When British shipowners learned that she had 1,118 tons of prime tea aboard, they were even more astonished at her carrying capacity. Why the *Oriental* was earning $14 per 40 cubic feet, while the most British ships could earn was $8.22.

Then and there the tea importers decided that they must build clippers for themselves. The American clippers would almost certainly have remained at the head of the race, but for the American Civil War, caused many American shippers to sell clippers to British firms, for fear of Confederate raiders such as the *Banshee* and the *Alabama*.

THE GREAT TEA RACE

So, the competition to see who could bring the new tea fastest from China was not an international event but a contest among British firms. Keen rivalry now began to develop. The first ship home in London river would sell her cargo of tea at a fancy price, while her captain and crew would receive a large bonus to share amongst them. The shipping companies began to order faster and faster ships, such as the first British clipper, *Stornoway,* built in Aberdeen. They would sail on the newly pioneered "great circle routes," which were elliptical courses plotted across the curved face of the globe, instead of along lines of latitude on a flat chart.

There might be seven or eight ships in the year's race, all of which had left the Canton River on the same tide. Often nothing would be heard of the competing ships, nor would they see one another till they reached the approaches to the Channel. In Mincing Lane, London, where the tea merchants had their offices, the tea importers would eagerly follow shifts in the wind indicated by a wind clock installed in the ceiling of their counting houses. When the pointer indicated "southwest," a mounted messenger would gallop off to the tea merchant's suburban villa, drag him out of bed, and tell him that a favorable wind could now bring his ship (whose approach had been signaled by telegraph) up Channel from the Downs.

Great crowds would gather as the tug brought the winning tea clipper up river to the dock. The air would be rent by the whistles of shipping in the river, and by the cheers of the crowd. Even the rather staid and respectable "samplers" (men who blended the tea) and tea merchants would throw their top hats into the air (and probably never see them again) as the cable was put ashore.

The most famous tea race took place on May 30, 1866, when *Ariel, Taeping, Fiery Cross,* and *Serica* left Chinese waters on the same tide. After ninety-eight days at sea, *Ariel* sighted the Bishop Rock Light in the

Scilly Islands, at the entrance to the Channel. As dawn broke, her officers and crew caught sight of *Taeping,* driving along behind them with all sails set in true clipper tradition. The two ships swept up-Channel together, making more than thirteen knots, and in the end the race was declared to be a draw, the captains sharing the prize as well as the premium of ten shillings a ton for the first cargo of new tea landed.

Seven years later *Ariel* disappeared on one of her passages, and critics said that although her lines were so fine as to enable her to ghost along with barely a breath of wind blowing, they had also made it easy to drive herself under when carrying a press of sail.

MECHANIZATION OF SHIPS

Meanwhile quite another kind of ship had assumed the dominion of the seas, the steamship, driven first by great paddlewheels in combination with sail, and then by the screw propeller. In 1854, John Elder of Britain had invented the expansion engine, which reused the steam that had passed through the first cylinder. By 1874 the revolutionary "triple expansion" steam engine was a workable possibility. As the steam passed out of the first cylinder it was taken up by a second, then a third, working three pistons for the price of the original cylinder full of steam. The triple-expansion engine halved the price of an Atlantic passage for passengers and freight. Not only did it drive ships twice as fast as previous engines, but the storage space once devoted to coal could now be used for freight as well.

Almost hand in hand with the new high-speed engines came refrigerated ships. In 1850, James Harrison, a Scottish-born Australian, invented an ether-compressor ice-making machine, designed as a hot-weather aid to Australian brewers. Within thirty years this early device had been so improved that a vessel called the *Strathleven* successfully carried a cargo of frozen meat all the way from Australia to the United Kingdom.

Soon such voyages became commonplace. The development of the freezing plant and the refrigerator ship, like the refrigerated railroad car, benefited chiefly the meat industry and meant prosperity for such developing nations as Argentina, Australia, and New Zealand. But there were other beneficiaries. Quite poor Europeans could now afford oranges from Spain and bananas from Central America. Coconuts, which were such cherished treasures in the Middle Ages that rich men had cups made of the shells mounted in gold, appeared in English markets in the 1830's, and by the 1890's were being given away at side shows — "coconut shies."

MECHANIZATION OF FOOD

Like his uncle before him, Napoleon III was interested in improving France's food supply and offered a prize for the successful production of a fat as appetizing, nutritious, and stable as butter. To this end, he caused a factory near Poissy to be put at the disposal of any such inventor. In 1869 a French chemist named Hippolyte Mège-Mouries patented something he called oleomargarine, "oil of pearls." The new product was made from fresh beef fat digested in sodium carbonate with pepsin.

The conservative French were not enthusiastic about oleomargarine, which in its original form was smelly and not very tasty, but Americans were. Introduced in the United States in 1874, it was soon being manufactured widely, experimented with, improved upon. Once producers had learned how to emulsify vegetable fats, they abandoned suet as a base and began to try out a variety of oils — peanut oil, coconut oil, even such exotics as babassu oil. Eventually they settled on a formula whose principal ingredients were cottonseed and soybean oils. The name was shortened to "margarine."

All this caused a great outcry from dairy farmers, and the new product had hardly appeared before the governments of twenty-two states passed discriminatory laws and taxes against it. (As late as 1950, it was illegal to sell it precolored; it came as a white block, accompanied by a packet of yellow coloring matter, which had to be kneaded into the fat product.) Nevertheless by 1876, Americans were exporting a million pounds of it annually.

Meanwhile other "improvements" were being made in food products, mostly for the sales of their looks. Prime Minister Benjamin Disraeli (1804 – 81) spent much of his political life fighting the adulteration of food. When he entered Parliament in 1837, pickles were a beautiful glowing green because they had been colored with copperas (crystallized ferrous sulphate, a poisonous substance). The bread was full of alum, chalk, or ammonium carbonate (all poisonous) to make it look whiter. The sweets in the candy store were colored red with arsenic (poisonous) while the rind of Gloucester cheese was given its tempting orange hue by the addition of red lead (poisonous).

If the British working man tried to assuage the poisonous nature of his milk (full of chalk and lime) with a glass of beer, he would probably find that there was more lime in that, to make it froth, and that the bitter taste, which ought to have been imparted by hops, had in fact been achieved by some kind of chemical bitters, such as aconite. In 1876 Disraeli put through the Sale of Food and Drugs Act, which opened the modern trend toward rigid inspection of food and drink.

In America such reform had to wait considerably longer, and even then it was given its impetus more or less by accident. In 1906, Upton Sinclair, a young Socialist, published what he thought by calling attention to the miseries of immigrant workers in America. Titled *The Jungle*, it was laid in the packing plants in Chicago, which it revealed as rat-infested cesspools of filth and danger, and its readers were so aghast at these revelations that they forgot all about the plight of immigrant workers.* Instead they swung political support to reformers who had been trying to pass a Pure Food and Drug Act and a Meat Inspection Act, and the bills became law in the same year the book was published. Today no meat can be sold in interstate commerce without a federal inspection stamp, indicating that the meat is fit for human consumption and was processed under sanitary conditions.

THE TROUBLES OF THE EUROPEAN FARMER

The meat and cereals, which the American farmer raised so cheaply by mechanical means on homestead land and which was hustled on fast freights to transatlantic ports and packed aboard steamers using triple-expansion engines, could now be sold cheaply in Europe as well. Many European farmers lost their livelihoods — Norwegians, for instance, who had been living a marginal existence since the days of the Vikings. All over Europe and Asia impoverished peasants sold out the little they had and headed for the emigrant ships, to resettle where farming offered a man a return for his labor.

Scandinavians and Germans settled the high cold prairies of Minnesota, Wisconsin, the Dakotas, to grow wheat and dairy cattle. Italians flocked to sunny California to produce wine. Japanese flooded into California, too, to become truck farmers, or into Hawaii to grow pineapple and sugar cane. Farm laborers drained out of England and Scotland into Canada, Australia, New Zealand — the new ''white dominions'' — to raise sheep and wheat for shipment back to the mother country in the new refrigerated ships.

*Commented the novel's rueful author: ''I aimed at the public's heart, and by accident I hit it in the stomach.''

European governments worried about this drain, and most tried to fight it by imposing tariffs on foods imported from overseas. Chancellor Otto von Bismarck of the new German Empire, himself a landowner, felt that it would be a betrayal of his own social class if he allowed fellow landowners to be ruined by cheap American food imports. Bismarck had another motive in wanting high tariffs. He wished to make himself financially independent of the support of the German Liberal Party, which had hitherto constituted a hindrance (albeit a slight one) on his militaristic ambitions. The Liberals advocated free trade, or the absence of tariffs, and with their downfall completed, Bismarck was able to impose heavy import duties on incoming food products. The *Junker* (landowning) class prospered from this, the absolutism of the Empire was strengthened, but the common people of Germany had to pay more for food.

In England too the Liberals were in favor of free trade, but though a Conservative government was in power, its leader was Benjamin Disraeli, who, as we have seen, had a deep sense of identification with the common man and his needs. "Protection," he said of food tariffs, "is not merely dead but damned." This put him into a difficult position, torn between the Conservative landowners who supported his party and his personal concern for the hungry industrial masses. When the crisis of imported American food loomed, Disraeli chose to sacrifice his party associates rather than the poor — the lesser of the "two nations" that divided his country. No import duties were imposed, and the English farmer and farm laborer suffered.

The crisis came in 1875, a time when there had been particularly bad harvests and when British cattle had been attacked by rinderpest or bovine typhus, a devastating continental disease. Many farmers were unable to pay their rents, and although many landowners agreed to forgo rents temporarily, thus absorbing some of the shock, it was not enough. More ruined farmers joined the trek to Canada and Australia.

BLOCKADE

Still, on the whole more people benefited from the technological advantages of the Transport Revolution than were hurt by it. But this could only last as long as the transport was uninterrupted. And when a city population in the millions drew its food from far-off places, a break in food transport could be very serious indeed.

The Germans first proved this when they laid siege to Paris in the

Franco-Prussian War. From September 19, 1870, to the following January 28, no supplies could get in or out of the beleaguered city (although statesman Leon Gambetta made a spectacular escape by balloon on October 8). At first, inhabitants believed that they had little to suffer from the siege, because enormous stocks of food had been brought into the city. But no system of rationing had been set up to oversee distribution and establish priorities, and as supplies dwindled, people lost their heads. Those who had money bought bread and fed it to their horses. Poorer people used the bread to feed rabbits and chickens. Soon the bread was exhausted, along with other stocks, and the inhabitants had to eat the rabbits, chickens, and horses (although horse meat is not an unusual dish in France). Cats, dogs, rats followed, and finally Parisians were eating the animals in the zoo.

Rationing was introduced finally, but too late. The death rate rose from the usual figure of 1,200 per week to 3,000, then 4,500. Finally, after only four short months of siege, the city was forced to surrender.

Forty-four years later the Germans tried to repeat their success in using hunger as an ally — not against a city but a whole nation. At the outset of World War I, Britain felt confident that, having the largest navy in the world, she could continue to draw her supplies of food from all the far continents. She had failed to note that the last decades had changed naval history by perfecting the submarine.

The German U-boats (short for *Untersee-boote*, "undersea boats") concentrated on the sea lanes near the south and west coasts of England — the chops of the Channel — and began the war politely enough. They surfaced at the approach of a merchantman, ascertained that it was indeed an enemy ship, then allowed the crew to leave in lifeboats before they sank it. But the British lost so many food vessels this way that the Admiralty took to arming them and sending them out with instructions to ram their attacker before it could fire a torpedo. Soon U-boats were firing without warning, and losses mounted.

Patrol of the sea lanes, the use of Q ships (armed decoys), destroyer screens, all helped combat the submarine but could not defeat it. The convoy system, a British invention, helped protect merchantmen against the "wolves of the sea," but the Royal Navy had too few patrol vessels to make it entirely effective. And in early 1917, the Germans declared their intention of opening unrestricted submarine warfare — that is, torpedoing all ships, neutral or not, caught in the war zones surrounding Britain. This was aimed particularly at the United States, the principal neutral shipper, and eventually it brought America into World War I.

But its immediate effect was to devastate Britain's already spreading scarcity of foodstuffs.

By the winter of 1916– 17, bread lines were seen in Midlands cities, and the government was forced to establish strict food controls. Meanwhile the shipping losses soared. From 103,000 tons a month in 1916, it leaped to 311,000 in February, 1917; 352,000 in March; and 526,000 in April. At one point there was just six weeks' supply of food left in the entire country.

Then the weight of the American entry began to tell — especially of the U.S. Navy with its large contribution of escort craft, needed to make the convoy system work — and gradually the submarine menace was brought under control. American Food Administrator Herbert Hoover bought up the entire American hog crop and sugar harvest and shipped it to the United Kingdom, and the day was saved. Indeed, the island kingdom emerged from the war the best-fed of all the European belligerents. But it had been a close call.

12.
Fruits Of The Earth

The last quarter of the nineteenth century was marked by one of those dramatic changes in the world's taste in food that we have noticed once or twice before in the past. It was almost as if man had moved back from the age of hunting to the age of food gathering. Instead of wanting to consume nothing but bread and meat, people in Western Europe and America suddenly became aware of the virtues that resided in vegetables and fruit.

VEGETARIANISM

Eating vegetables and fruit was not a new departure. Whole civilizations have been vegetarian. In India, for instance, people live exclusively on rice, vegetables, and dairy products. Before 1853 Japan, a Buddhist country, had abstained completely from meat. However, the Japanese ate a lot of fish, on the grounds that fish are not warm-blooded creatures, so that it is not against the Buddhist creed to kill and eat them.

Though the determination not to live through the destruction of one's fellow creatures is a high-minded ideal, dieticians have always been doubtful about the benefits of a strict vegetarian diet. Monks in a Japanese Buddhist monastery, for example, tend to suffer from such diseases as beri-beri — a deficiency disease caused by lack of vitamin B. Indians who live on a wholly vegetable diet are not notable either for high productivity or good health. When, around 1853, the Japanese took to Western ways, including eating meat, their health probably improved, while their average height certainly went up by an inch or so.

Yet in the last quarter of the nineteenth century, many people became, if not wholly vegetarian, at least larger consumers of vegetables and fruits than heretofore. It was the era of the great Russian scientist Ilya Metchnikoff, who assured his followers that meat released poisons into the blood during digestion. Consequently a greater intake of fruit could only promote health.

The increased consumption of fruit was not just due to deliberate choice. More fruit became available, not merely the ordinary fruits that people had consumed for centuries, but much more exotic ones, which for most people had hitherto existed only in travelers' tales. The production of fruit and vegetables for the world market gave rise to "monocultures" — specialized farming by many countries and several parts of America, to supply the newly acquired tastes.

FRUIT IN THE NEW WORLD

America had always been closely associated with fruit, because the first name by which it became known to the outside world was "Vinland" or "land of grapes."

This name had been given to it by the Viking explorer Leif Ericsson, who discovered it. While he was encamped on the shore of what modern historians believe to have been Newfoundland, his foster father, a German, went out exploring and returned with news that the island teemed with wild grapes — hence the name.

The Pilgrim Fathers found many fruits growing in New England when they arrived: blueberries (which incidentally are cultivated only in the United States and Canada), cranberries, huckleberries, crab apples, raspberries, wild plums, several varieties of wild cherry, and many others.

"We cannot set down a foot but we tread on strawberries," a colonist from Maryland wrote home to England, referring to the wild strawberry, (*Fragaria virginiana*). The Pilgrims found several species of plums; in fact the plum is the most widely distributed wild fruit tree in America.

But the colonists were not content to rely on just the fruits they found in America. They tried to establish all the fruit trees they had grown in

England, not just for food but because they were thus reminded of home.

They brought with them, for instance, the pear tree, which was going to thrive in the New World as it never had in England. In the most famous of all colonial fruit nurseries, Prince Nursery on Long Island, no fewer than forty-two varieties of pear were growing in 1771. Captain John Smith reported from Virginia in 1629 that the apricot was flourishing there, too, although the East Coast climate is not considered suitable for apricot growing today. Peaches, however, another fruit introduced in colonial days, were a great success; peach orchards became a favorite with colonists, particularly in the South, for they were the source of peach brandy. Almonds, figs, walnuts, and other exotics were introduced as well.

But the fruit to which they were most emotionally committed — which became and remains the favorite American fruit — was the apple. Orchards were soon blooming fragrantly wherever English settlements had been made, and spread westward along with the tide of settlement. Indians adopted the crunchy red fruit and planted orchards of their own. In the early nineteenth century, an itinerant Swedenborgian preacher named John Chapman made it his mission in life to plant apple orchards all up and down the Ohio valley; wherever he wandered, orchards bloomed from seeds obtained from the discards of cider mills. He is known to history and American folklore as Johnny Appleseed. From these small beginnings — a favorite type of fruit tree, brought over from England and lovingly watered with water saved from the skimpy ship's ration — have developed the great fruit industries of modern America: apple orchards such as those of the Pacific Northwest, New York, and Ohio, the cherry orchards of Michigan, and the vast fruit-growing industry of California. It was not these home-grown fruits, which had become "as American as apple pie" that were going to catch world imagination, however, but more exotic produce — to grown in the hot, humid climate of the American tropics.

THE EXOTICS

Although by the last half of the nineteenth century, everyone had heard of tropical fruits, but only a very few rich and influential people were privileged to taste them. If people in general had known, no doubt they too would have exclaimed, as did Disraeli: "There is nothing so delicious as a banana."

Travelers had waxed eloquent about eating such fruits and about the beauty of their appearance. They knew that health improved enormously if such fruits were added to the diet. They eliminated scurvy and many other ills, because — as scientists were to prove in the early twentieth century — they were rich in vitamin C. It was tragically ironical that, in 1912, just when the connection between scurvy and vitamin C was becoming scientifically established, British explorer Robert Falcon Scott and his whole expedition were to perish of scurvy. A few tins of Florida orange juice would have saved the entire South Pole expedition.

Tropical fruits, such as the avocado, banana, breadfruit, cashew apple, coconut, fig, grapefruit, guava, jujube, kumquat, lime, mango, muskmelon, papaya, pineapple, pomegranate, pomelo, tamarind, and watermelon were known to the average Westerner only from pictures or books.

Very few Europeans were able to eat watermelon and pineapple, raised in hothouses built for the purpose. George III grew pineapples at Kew, and at Kew there was also a fine orangery, a brick house with tall glass windows heated by steam pipes and housing orange trees in tubs on wheels. In the summer the orange trees were wheeled outside into the sunshine, and when autumn came, back they went inside the orangery.

Some tropical fruits had been established in Europe for so long that people thought of them as native European plants and trees. The orange, of South China and Indochina, origin had been successfully established in Spain, Portugal, and other sunny European countries. The lemon, which came from the southern Himalayas, northern Burma, and eastern India, had undergone the same process, as had the lime, native to Burma. In consequence the citrus family became the first European fruits to become established in America, for Columbus sowed orange, lime, and lemon pips in his colony of Hispaniola (Haiti) in 1493. He had brought them from Gomera, in the Canaries, along with those of other plants.

The movement of oranges and lemons from one country to another was followed by that of many other tropical fruits. In their modern form they are almost as much the work of man as of nature. The process began when some dedicated plant collector noticed by a tasty new fruit, often in some remote part of the world. It would be sent home and planted in some public or private garden and then undergo a long process of selection and cultivation to improve its characteristic qualities.

The pomelo had been introduced into the West Indies from the East Indies by a certain Captain Shaddock in the latter half of the seventeenth century. Shaddock may also have introduced the ''forbidden fruit'' or grapefruit, first described by naturalist Griffith Hughes on Barbadoes in the eighteenth century, but botanists are not agreed as to whether it was introduced separately or developed as a "sport" or mutation of the pomelo, which today is often called a shaddock.

The grapefruit was only one fruit that arrived in new surroundings as part of the to-and-fro of colonization. The banana had originated in India, where it was known as "the fruit of the wise." Presumably Indian yogas and ascetics ate it green, as a proof of austerity, just as Christian anchorites and monks did in Abyssinia until recently. It was introduced into Hispaniola from the Canary Islands by Friar Tomas de Berlanga, a Spanish missionary priest, in 1516. Shortly afterward the plant reached Mexico, where it thrived as if it were native to the country.

The avocado, also known as alligator pear, was a staple food of the Aztecs and Mayas, and was introduced into northern South America long before the Europeans arrived. The name comes from the Aztec *ahuacatl*. Early settlers of the United States were rather conservative in their food tastes, and although the avocado was native to North American it was not cultivated there till 1833, when Henry Perrine, a well-known horticulturist, established it south of Miami, with plants imported from Mexico. The papaya, a relative of the avocado, also an American fruit, has never caught on in America at all. It is widely grown in Africa, and I often ate it for breakfast, with lemon juice, though I must confess I found it rather tasteless. It contains an enzyme, papain, which has the property of tenderizing tough meat, and today it is grown extensively for use in commercial tenderizers.

One reason why the papaya has never established itself as a delicacy in great demand is that the fruit can be very big, as much as twenty pounds weight. So it is impracticable except for a hotel or restaurant proprietor to buy papayas.

Mangoes, a native of southeast Asia and the Malay Archipelago, were also introduced into America by horticulturist Henry Perrine, in 1833, but the trees he planted south of Miami were lost and the fruit had to be reintroduced.

Not all the tropical fruits popular today were imported into America. Some are native, such as the guava, the custard apple, cashew apple, and pineapple. The pineapple, an important American fruit, was discovered in its native home, Brazil or possibly Paraguay. The French name for pineapple, *ananas,* is much more apt than our own, since it comes from two words in the Guarani Indian language meaning "an excellent fruit," as the pineapple certainly is.

The sapodilla, another homebred American fruit, has become famous because it is the raw material for chewing gum. For centuries the Mayas of Central America boiled down the sticky, milk-white latex of the wild sapodilla tree to make the chicle used in chewing gum. Europeans had chewed gum before being introduced to chicle, but it was mastic gum from the Greek islands.

BREADFRUIT SAGA

The tropics produce many more varieties of fruit than have become established in the diet of ordinary Americans or Europeans. Sometimes these "unadopted" fruits are hard to grow, sometimes there are marketing difficulties, as in the case of the papaya. But usually the reason for indifference to certain fruit is sheer conservative eating habits.

The breadfruit, best known of all colonial transplantations, is a case in point. In 1787 Lt. William Bligh sailed to Tahiti, picked up a cargo of breadfruit seedlings, and set out for the West Indies. There the canny West Indian planters hoped that, if they planted breadfruit, they would be able to feed their slaves on the produce, without bothering to give them anything else.

On the voyage from Tahiti to the Caribbean, Bligh's crew mutinied and set him and a few loyal companions adrift in a small boat, never expecting Bligh to make land. Incredibly, he did, after one of the longest voyages ever made in an open boat, and in 1791, he completed his mission, establishing the breadfruit in the Caribbean.

The West Indian slaves, however, aware that introducing it was just an attempt to feed them at minimum expense, refused to eat the bread. Then came emancipation. The planters had expected that the freed slaves would go on working in the sugar fields as free laborers. But the slaves now awakened to the virtues of the Polynesian tree, virtues which Lord Byron summed up in some lines of poetry.

The bread-tree, which without the ploughshare yields,
The unreaped harvest of unfurrowed fields
And bakes its unadulterated loaves,
Without a furnace in unpurchased groves,
And flings off famine from its fertile breast,
A priceless market for the gathering guest.

The former slaves realized that they had no need to work for a living — they could keep themselves and their families by what was called in the West Indies *la petite culture,* or small-time husbandry. The great German naturalist Alexander von Humboldt had pointed out that just a tiny plot of fruit trees and plants around a cabin in the forest would allow the tropical farmer to grow enough food to keep his family. More than thirty-three times more nourishment could be grown in this way than if he were growing wheat, so productive were the tropical fruits and vegetables.

BANANAS IN THE CARIBBEAN

Unfortunately for the idea of self-sufficiency, man does not live by bread alone. He requires all sorts of other goods and services, the advice of a doctor, for example. What was more, the very availability of food tends to push up the population level, as it did in the farmer sugar islands.

The Caribbean sank into poverty and economic doldrums. As if to emphasize the stagnation of commerce and industry, the principal coin in circulation remained the Spanish doubloon of buccaneer days, worth about $1.50.

Then in the 1860's, the economic apathy of the West Indies was stirred by a sudden new demand — for tropical fruit. In 1866 a Captain Busch, owner of a small sailing vessel, the *Raymond,* took a few bunches of bananas from Port Antonio, Jamaica, to Boston, Massachusetts. This small shipment proved so profitable that in 1869 Busch formed a company to carry on regular shipping of fruit to America.

So the banana industry was born, and on the larger and smaller islands of the Caribbean, which had been suffering from unemployment, civil disturbances, and direct-grant aid from the parent country, a wind of change began to blow.

Captain Lorenzo Dow Baker, a Cape Cod skipper who had heard of the profits to be made in fruit, took his eighty-five-ton schooner *Telegraph* into Port Morant, Jamaica, on June 2, 1870. In a week he had loaded a cargo of bananas and coconuts, with which he sailed for New Jersey. He reached port on June 23, having made a very good passage, and sold his cargo at an enormous profit. One reason for his profit was the short duration of the voyage. Bananas must be cut green and ripen at a special temperature. If they are delayed, chilled, or overheated, they go rotten — as many other skippers besides Dow had discovered.

Trusting to his luck, the bewhiskered Cape Codder decided to take up the banana business as a full-time occupation. He returned to Jamaica with a cargo of flour, pork, salt cod, printed cottons, and "Yankee notions." Once again he made a big profit on his shipment of bananas and coconuts, and soon he was sailing around the Caribbean, persuading the Jamaicans to produce more "green gold."

In 1885 Baker founded the Boston Fruit Company to buy bananas from local growers and import them into the United States in specially insulated ships. But he soon began to see that the real money lay in controlling the entire industry — planting, growing, picking, shipping. He first established plantations of his own in Jamaica and Cuba, then began to look around for new worlds to conquer. He chose Panama, where an American businessman named Minor Keith had built a railroad and laid out some banana farms of his own. In 1899 Keith and Baker founded a new venture, the United Fruit Company, and set out to make "Central America" and "banana" well-nigh synonymous. They succeeded so well that by 1920 bananas were the economic prop of Panama, Costa Rica, Guatemala, Nicaragua, parts of Colombia and Mexico, and above all Honduras.

The UFC brought much modernization into Central America — sanitation, medical care, port facilities, electricity, water-supply systems, sewerage, housing, schools — but it also interfered blatantly in local politics, siding with those political parties that promised special treatment, agreeing to build roads in return for tax concessions and then never building them, and so on. By the 1950's, resentment against foreign fruit companies, especially UFC, caused widespread unrest among native peoples and was one of the running grievances that today are leading the region into revolution.

THE HOTHOUSE OF EUROPE

In the Canaries, just as in the West Indies earlier, good fruit was going to waste by the ton, food for the hungry masses of the industrial cities and also for the better-to-do in England and Europe, who were tired of traditional fare, with its emphasis on heavy meat eating.

The Canary Islanders grew bananas, but only for food, not as a market crop. They fed cattle on the banana leaves and stems, and used their manure to fertilize the land. Farming is not an easy business in the Canaries, as the volcanoes dominate the landscape. In the past they have often erupted, burying fields in lava several feet deep. Undaunted, the Canarians back-packed loads of new soil onto the lava and created fresh fields. To hold the scarce moisture of the windy islands, they surround each onion plant with a windbreak, and scatter volcanic scoria over the surface of the soil. This acts as an insulator, keeping the moisture of the dew within reach of the plant roots. Water is so scarce in the islands that anyone who lives on even a barren watershed, down which rainwater will flow, is a comparatively rich man. For years the islanders have been constructing a complex system of terraces, irrigation conduits, and dams to bring water to their fields.

Such were the hard-working people who were struck by an economic disaster when, in 1853, phylloxera, a variety of plant lice, destroyed the vines from which they grew their Canary wine. The islanders rallied and instead began raising cochineal beetles (used to obtain a red dye) on cactus plants. Then the invention of aniline dyes ruined the cochineal industry.

The demand for bananas and other fruits and vegetables came as a godsend to the Canarians. Instead of plowing back their unwanted bananas, they began to sell them to a new fruit importer who had just become active on the islands in the 1870's — Thomas Fyffe. In a short time the Canaries had become what they have since remained, the hothouse of Europe. They raise the early vegetables that Europeans enjoy in the spring, and they also raise the fruit that is eaten in Europe all year round. Although they now have tourism to fall back on, the Canary Islands are still very delicately poised, like most ''single crop'' countries. They are very dependent on the weather, and as there is no other outlet for their fruit and vegetables except Europe, they are very much in the power of their wholesalers. There is always the possibility that market demands may lead to overproduction — thus exhausting the soil — or a drop in demand may force the growers to cut back their crops.

Whereas Captain Baker had simply loaded his bananas into the hold, Thomas Fyffe achieved the first success in controlling the temperature of the fruit in transit. He was the agent for a fleet of English coaling ships, and as these went back to England empty, he was able to secure cheap passage for his fruit. He got around the problem of temperature by packing the fruit in cotton wool and storing it in open crates on deck. At the equable temperature at which the bananas traveled, these would arrive in England still green and be ripened before they were sold.

It is one thing to take a horse to water, it is another to make it drink. Did the English really want bananas? The task of turning the British public as a whole into banana eaters was largely the work of one of Fyffe's successors, Henry Arthur Stockley. Stockley was related on his mother's side to the Christian family, from which had come Fletcher

Christian, the leader of the *Bounty*'s mutineers. Stockley threw himself into the business of popularizing the new fruit, and while it was catching on, acquired a new fleet. They were special ships fitted with refrigeration, apparently the first ever used for shipping fruit. The Fyffe ships began to operate a speedy and punctual schedule from the West Indies to London. Never had fruit traveled so far so quickly, and on such a tight schedule.

On March 18, 1901, after a thirteen-day crossing which was almost a record for this type of ship, the 2,831-ton *Port Morant* docked in Avonmouth, Gloucestershire, England, with Britain's first consignment of Jamaica bananas. So quick had been the transit that the astonished dockers found all sorts of live creatures in the bunches of bananas: birds' nests with eggs, tarantulas, and even little bright-eyed opossums, which fetched a big price at the quayside.

British wholesalers and the railways were deeply suspicious of Stockley's new imports. There were no refrigerator vans available, and the wholesalers were not prepared to ripen the fruit. Stockley bypassed them and sold directly to a kind of retail fruit dealer who perhaps deserves a word of introduction.

The costermongers, or costers, were fruit salesmen who carried their wares around the streets in donkey carts. They got their name from costard, an English cooking apple, and they were famous for their special way of dressing — corduroy trousers, cut very wide, and jackets of the same material, with a silk neckerchief and visored cap. Few costers ever had any money. They would start the day's trading by borrowing fifty cents from the coster moneylenders. They would then buy the fruit, sell it, and hand the moneylender back sixty cents at night. This represents an interest of 7,000 percent. Yet, though the moneylenders got rich, the costers did not starve. At the end of the day they would be left with a profit of forty cents. With this profit, a coster would feed his donkey, or "moke," keep his wife and children, and regale himself with pints of beer at half a cent a pint. The persuasive patter of the costers soon convinced their customers that they were buying the food of the rich at the price of the poor, which indeed they were.

Mangoes, which like the bananas were first introduced into Europe by Fyffe, had once cost $4.32 *wholesale* from high-society fruiterers. Now that Fyffe began to import them into England by the ton, anyone could afford them. Likewise the banana. In 1901 a beggar knocked on the door of a clergyman in Bristol, Gloucestershire, and asked for a handout. The clergyman gave him a banana, whereupon the beggar, becoming very indignant, said he could buy bananas anywhere for half a cent each. He knocked the clergyman down.

FRUIT EMPIRES IN THE UNITED STATES

If tropical fruit could make the fortune of the Caribbean, might it not do the same for those parts of America where it could be raised? There were factors both for and against the establishment of a fruit empire in the United States. Alone among Western people, Americans ate fruit for breakfast. English breakfasts might include eggs, kedgeree (fish cooked with butter and curry powder and served with rice), cold grouse, deviled kidneys, bacon and sausages, porridge, toast, muffins, coffee, and tea, but they never included fruit. In Europe fruit was served as a dessert.

Americans had also been somewhat conservative about adopting the new fruits. Avocados had not been planted in Santa Barbara, California, till 1871, though they grew across the border in Mexico. In early days the tomato was much better known and appreciated in Europe than in America. As late as the early nineteenth century, Fitz Hugh Lane, the very talented New England seascape artist, could assure his friends that his semi-paralyzed condition was due to his having eaten a "Peru apple" (tomato) as a child. (Lane's crippled condition was actually due to polio, but his belief in such a story is an indication of the common mistrust of this fruit.)

The great breakthrough to fruit growing in America (other than the old staples such as apples and plums) came with the arrival of immigrants who had experienced growing tropical and semitropical fruits in their own lands. Entire states in America such as Florida, California, and Hawaii, became fruit farms.

In Florida, grapefruit had been introduced by Don Philippe, a Spanish nobleman, to Safety Harbor, on Tampa Bay, about 1840. For the subsequent few decades grapefruit was hardly known elsewhere. Then, after 1880, some northern shipments of the fruit began. By the end of the century the grapefruit was still so much a rarity as to attract comment when served at table. In 1910, production reached a million boxes a year.

The orange got an early start in Florida. It may have reached there even before it was planted at St. Augustine, which was settled in 1565.

The Indians realized its value and planted it around their villages.* On the sites of these once flourishing villages, wild groves of oranges sprang up: one, discovered in 1764, was forty miles long.

Unlike other tropical imports, the mandarin orange was brought to Florida quite early. It had arrived in New Orleans, planted there by the Italian consul, between 1840 and 1850, about the same time that it reached Europe.

Commercial orange growing got off to a shaky start in Florida, having been launched after 1821, when the area first became part of the United States. Just as the groves were getting well started, along came the massive freeze of 1835, which killed off all the orange trees in Florida except for one grove on Merritt Island, located just off the warm sea inlet known as Indian River. Cuttings from this one grove reestablished the industry throughout the state, and in time the Indian River area became famous as the home of one of the world's finest oranges, often bought specially for royal tables.

From time to time, Florida has suffered other killing frosts, notably in 1895 and 1962. Modern growing techniques have helped to offset the losses incurred from these national disasters, however. Florida's low-lying topography and hot damp climate help produce thin-skinned juicy fruit, and thus it has become the home of the orange-juice industry. California, by contrast, whose climate is much drier, produces thick-skinned fruit, sweet and comparatively juiceless, considered "eating oranges." Florida grows nearly three times as much citrus fruit as her rival.

But California is not subject to frosts as serious as those of Florida, and consequently it has earned an enviable reputation as a center for orchards and truck farms of all sorts. The Spanish padres, who were the first intensive fruit growers, had an eye for good land, and always sited their missions in areas favorable to orchards. They grew lemons, figs, oranges, grapes, and olives. Indian converts helped the fathers dig the irrigation ditches that the fruit needed.

By the nineteenth century irrigation and fruit growing were in full swing in California. The great San Joaquin and Kings River Canal had been begun in 1871, the biggest venture of its kind since the cutting of the Erie Canal in New York State. As the Gold Rush swept through California in the 1850's, many would-be miners gave up prospecting to become fruit growers. One sent to Brazil for navel orange seedlings. They arrived by way of Washington. Two of the original seedlings are

---

*The Seminoles are still a primary supplier of Rough Lemon seeds, a variety of citrus on which most Florida oranges are grown. The fruit grows wild in the Everglades.

now sturdy trees in the Mission Inn garden in Riverside. The others have spread throughout California.

By 1894 California's 13,000 growers had formed their own Fruit Exchange, whose "Sunkist" brand became known throughout the world. California's remoteness from Eastern markets ended with the coming, around 1900, of the refrigerated car and the refrigerated ship. Soon the Golden State was shipping out 100,000 carloads of oranges a year, each car traveling an average of 2,600 miles. Orange picking never ceased; navels were picked from December to May and Valencias the rest of the year. Europe took upward of a million boxes of oranges a year, and by the mid-1930's California had picked and sold fruit valued at $2 billion, more than the worth of all the gold mined in the state since the first strike at Sutter's Mill.

By the same date more empty yellow cars could be seen assembled in railroad switchyards and sidings during the winter than would have moved the whole American army in World War I. They were waiting for the seasonal lettuce, peas, cantaloupes, cauliflower, celery, and other vegetables to make their way east. Below sea level, the Imperial Valley grew more cantaloupes, honeydews, and casaba melons than any area of its size in the world.

Fruit not only spelled prosperity for California, but publicized the message that, at a time when people were trying to get to America, everyone in America wanted to go to California. Settlers poured in to the accompaniment of rate wars between the Southern Pacific and Santa Fe lines. On a particularly bitter day of strife one could buy a ticket from Kansas City to the Coast for only a dollar!

PINEAPPLE KINGDOM

If citrus fruit spelled prosperity for California and Florida the pineapple certainly made Hawaii's fortune. The hilly and rainly archipelago of Hawaii was discovered by Captain James Cook in 1778. Like the other islands of the eastern Pacific, it was inhabited by Polynesians, a tall, fine-looking, noble race scourged by addiction to petty wars and cannibalism. On his second visit to the islands, early in 1779, Cook was killed in a skirmish with the inhabitants and partly eaten by them.

Early in the 1800's sperm whales began to use Hawaii as a port of call. In an attempt to evangelize the Hawaiians and to minimize the evil effects of contact with the whalers, a number of American missionaries left New England and settled in Honolulu, tolerated by King

Kamehameha II on condition that they teach his people to read and write. A small colony of Americans thus became the first non-Hawaiian group to settle on the islands. They and their descendants built churches and set up businesses. Eventually they helped to lead the revolution that overthrew Queen Liliuokalani in 1893, and led to annexation by the American government in 1898.

When the Stars and Stripes were first officially raised on Hawaii, the principal crop was sugar, which had developed from sugarcane cast away on the islands after the shipwreck of a Chinese junk. Pineapples, originally native to South America but widely cultivated around the world, were imported from the East Indies, but they succeeded so well that the growers could not make a profit from them. You could buy a hundred pineapples for a dollar. In despair, the planters rooted them out and grew other crops. A few were saved for kitchen gardens.

This was the state of affairs when Sanford B. Dole, a Honolulu-born Harvard graduate, decided to make pineapple into, not a local crop, but an international one, which could be canned and sent overseas to the United States. Dole had no capital, but like his contemporary, John D. Rockefeller, he was very persuasive. Borrowing enough to start a canning business, he also set out pineapple plantations on Oahu, introduced the Cayenne pineapple from America, and got to work.

Pineapple growing bristled with difficulties. The fruit was protected by sharp, spiny leaves, so that the gatherer had to wear heavy gloves and leggings to protect himself from the sawtooth edges. Pineapples favor loose soil, good drainage, and lots of moisture. Here the heavy rainfall of Hawaii was a great help. The fruit was planted on the upper ranges of the hills, leaving the lower levels for sugarcane. In areas where water was scarce, tunnels brought it from thirty miles away, and the pineapples were planted through sheets of porous paper, called mulch paper. Where mulch paper was used, it conserved every drop of moisture by soaking it up like a blotter, while at the same time it protected the tender roots of the plants from the tropic sun and stopped the growth of weeds. By the time the paper had disintegrated and blown away, the pineapple was well established.

Dole's pickers, recruited from China, Scandinavia, Japan, Madeira, Puerto Rico, Portugal, the Philippines, and Indiana, moved in on the first crop, picking the fruit, dropping it into gunny sacks and then transferring the burden to forty-pound lug boxes, which had to be heaved onto trucks.

Dole had begun in 1903 by exporting 2,000 cases of canned pineapples. Within a few years, his cannery was turning out as much as that in fifteen minutes. Soon the entire pineapple was being put to use. The juice, which had once been drained into the harbor and discolored the water, was being canned as well, doubling the business. Pineapple shells were dried and used as cattle feed, while citric acid from the sliced fruit became a major by-product.

Once, a pineapple had been the rarest fruit treasure imaginable. Charles II had even called one of his mistresses, a Miss Palmer, "pineapple." Now, thanks to Dole, the fruit of kings had become a commonplace and in the process the bustling, prosperous, multiracial community of Hawaii had been created.

13.

Food And Famine

Like the quest for food itself, famine has had a great deal to do with shaping human destinies. Famines have been commonplace throughout history. Between 100 B.C. and A.D. 1910, China experienced no fewer than 1,800 famines. India, too, has suffered innumerable devastating famines, notably an eleven-year dearth in the twelfth century, the ghastly "skull" famine of 1790 – 92 when the dead lay unburied, and the terrible scenes in Bangladesh as recently as the 1970's.

CAUSES OF FAMINE

Famines could result from any number of causes: a succession of bad harvests, a change for the worse in climate, wars that interrupt the business of sowing and reaping, a breakdown in the normal arrangements for transport (a flood washing out roads and bridges, a hard freeze in areas where supplies move by water transport or, conversely, an unseasonal thaw in countrysides that rely on sledges for heavy hauling, heavy seas isolating an island community for weeks at a stretch). Other factors include the deliberate destruction of food supplies by war raiders or religious fanatics; the vanishing or migration of animal species on which a society depends; population outstripping food production; the spread of some plant, animal, or human disease; devastation by insects, drought, and, as we have seen, blockade by the enemy.

Often famines break out for unknown reasons. The great dearths of the Middle Ages, caused by frequent failures of the wheat crop, were only explained in the twentieth century, when scientists identified the culprit as a plant disease transmitted from barberry bushes. The Arabs introduced barberry to the Mediterranean area, because its bright berries were considered both medicinal and an ingredient in conserve. Unfortunately the barberry was host to the parasite black-stem rust, which also attacked wheat.

Rye was likewise victimized by plant disease, a fungus called ergot. If ergot-infested rye is eaten, it causes the disease ergotism, the chief symptom of which is a construction of the blood vessels.* The victim suffers burning pain, gangrene, blackening of the extremities, and death when the respiratory muscles are affected. The burning pain caused medieval people to name it Saint Anthony's fire.

There were many minor outbreaks of ergotism throughout the Middle Ages and several major ones, notably in 944 and 1090 in eastern France. The same area suffered an epidemic of the disease as late as 1816, and isolated cases still occur.

EFFECTS OF FAMINE

The reaction to famine by those who suffer from it is often very violent. Cannibalism frequently occurs. Indeed the very existence of cannibalism may be a sort of insurance against famine. Cannibalism is not just a ''savage'' practice. Anyone can become a cannibal. Thus cannibalism is reported from many localities where it has been induced purely by famine, such as in Germany during the Thirty Years War. And the experiences of people marooned in the mountains by snow — the Donner party in the Sierras in the winter of 1846 – 47, and the airplane survivors in the Andes in the 1960's, to name two — show that, when it is a matter of life or death, men can overcome their aversion to eating human flesh.

Another predictable reaction to famine is a violent attack on the local government. Famines are often contributing causes to revolution, the French Revolution being the best-known example. Even a one-crop famine can have important political results, if the sufferers choose to

Ergot is still employed as a drug to control bleeding and sometimes as an abortifacient.

vent their frustration on their leader. This is what happened in France in the 1860's when an infestation of the plant louse phylloxera devastated the French vineyards. Hitherto French peasants had been among the strongest supporters of the Emperor Napoleon III, but now, blaming the government for doing nothing to stop the disaster, the peasants abandoned Napoleon, and when he was overthrown in 1870, made no attempt to rally to his aid.

A very common reaction to famine, or the threat of famine, is the offering of human sacrifices. The Aztecs sacrificed 15,000 people annually to appease the gods and ensure that the natural rhythms of nature be carried on — the sunrise, the rainfall, and the earth-given nourishment. Thus males were slaughtered on the top of a pyramid, women beheaded while they danced, and children drowned as an offering to the rain god Tlaloc. Because most of the sacrificial victims were prisoners of war, the Aztecs lived in a perpetual state of war with their neighbors.

It was the same story in ancient China. During the Shang Dynasty (1500 – 1030 B.C.) the Chinese believed that human sacrifices were necessary to promote the fertility of the earth. Wars were undertaken just to get prisoners for the imperial sacrifices, while the common people, who had the same beliefs as their rulers, lurked near springs to waylay innocent travelers and then sacrificed them to ensure a good harvest, burying parts of their bodies in the fields.

Some of the effects of famine have already been noted. They include the extinction of whole peoples, such as the rather advanced Eskimo civilizations, which at one time flourished around the Bering Strait and then simply disappeared when the seal and walrus population either moved or was wiped out. Then there is the overthrow of governments, wars undertaken to obtain food, and the movement of whole peoples in search of food. Some historians have argued that famines can have a long-range beneficial effect. By killing off the elderly and weaker part of the population, they leave a young, healthy group of survivors, who will produce vigorous and healthy children. In England the great population boom of the last quarter of the eighteenth century has even been interpreted as a swing back to normal after the higher mortality of the preceding century.

But for those who live through the haunting horrors of dearth, there is no such detached consolation. Consider the great Irish Potato Famine of 1845 – 48.

THE GREAT HUNGER

In 1842 a disease called late blight attacked and destroyed the potatoes along the Atlantic coast from Nova Scotia to Boston. It was caused by a parasitic fungus named *Phytophthora infestans*, which thrives in cool moist air. Late blight begins when black lesions, bordered underneath with white mildew, appear on the leaves of the potato plant. The skin of the tubers — whether in the ground or in storage — becomes discolored with brown or purple, followed by a dry rot that spreads into the flesh. Soon the entire plant is rotted and stinking, and the spores that spread the fungus are carried by the wind to the next plant, the next farmer's field.

Shortly after the Atlantic Coast outbreak, there was a similar attack on European potato fields, and in 1845 late blight reached Ireland. (It is presumed that the spores arrived by way lumber shipments from America to Great Britain). In Ireland it encountered a land where the potato was a way of life.

The Irish lived on buttermilk, potatoes, and whiskey. How they contrived to stay healthy on a diet of this sort is something of a mystery, but they did. The men were noted for their strength and manly appearance, the girls for their good looks. The climate probably had a lot to do with this. Ireland is a land of "fine soft mornings" of misty rain, mild winters and warm summers — in fact, a climate diametrically opposite to that of Peru, the native home of the potato.

The Irish did a little cultivation of the potato at springtime and harvest, and the rest of the year was their own. An abundance of cheap food and free fuel — the turf (peat) of the surrounding countryside — had encouraged an enormous population increase. Disraeli once declared that Ireland was the most populous country in Europe, with a population density on agricultural land that was higher than China's. Much of the potato crop was raised by a method of sharecropping called *conacre*. The potato grower would hire a patch of ground from a landlord and raise a crop on it, paying a very substantial rent for the privilege. On the potato the Irish family lived, while its peelings went to nourish hens and a pig, which was usually sold to pay the rent, as was any wheat that the farmer managed to grow.

Even in the best of times potato cultivation resulted in a hungry time of the year, June, July, and August, when the old potatoes had run out and the new had not yet appeared. The peasants then had to buy meal on credit from the "gombeen-man," the local petty dealer and usurer.

EMERGENCY MEASURES

Although the British government was vaguely aware that there might be a famine of considerable dimensions in Ireland someday, they had taken no steps against the catastrophe when it came. The whole country was backward — few harbors, bad roads — so that even to distribute relief supplies would be hampered by transport problems. Not that the government did plan to hand out free food.

As famine broke out in 1845, the English Civil Service attempted to ease matters as best it could, by shipping corn to Ireland to be sold to those whose potato crops had failed. Corn had been deliberately chosen because there was no trade in that product in the United Kingdom. The relief commissioners did not want to compete against existing grain merchants, much less to undercut their sales on the market.

Unfortunately it as flint corn, which was so hard that it had to be ground between water-driven millstones before it could be used. Mills were scarce in this country that lived on potatoes, and during a hot spell the streams dried up and rendered those few useless. Thus there were long delays before the corn could be made usable. Even so, the Irish were revulsed by "Peel's brimstone." Gradually it was borne in on the relief commissioners that this system was not working. Not only was corn unpopular, but the Irish had little money available to buy it, and that little they wanted to hold on to as rent for their little conacre plots. It was bad enough to be hungry, but if they failed to pay their rent, they would be driven out to die in a ditch.

Most of the landowners in Ireland were either English or nonresident Irish aristocrats, whose lands were managed for them in their absence by bailiffs. Under pressure from these absentee landlords, bailiffs were always having to raise the rents — "rack renting," it was called — and they did not hesitate to evict tenants who could not pay. One of the most distressing features of the Great Hunger was the appearance of many homeless wanderers on the roads, gaunt and half-dead, whose cottages had been pulled down around their ears.

To modern eyes the most obvious action for the commissioners to take was distribution of free food. But the government didn't want to do that, because of opposition from England, where people similarly pauperized were forced to go and live in the workhouses provided in each parish.

Until 1834 a large proportion of the English population had been living on poor relief. According to this system, anyone who was unemployed or poorly paid could have his income adjusted so that he and his family could afford the minimum amount of food to keep life together — one loaf per week made from three gallons of flour (more bread than most people eat in a month) for a man, and half that for a woman.

Under this system of "outdoor" relief — that is, handed out to people not living in an institution — Britain had been pauperized, the burden on the taxpayer intolerable. So in 1834 outdoor relief was ended. From then on, if a family was destitute, it could only obtain relief by entering the parish workhouse (poorhouse). Thus, if direct relief was given to the starving Irish, there would have been an outcry from the English poor against this "favoritism."

Yet something had to be done. People were living on nettles and weeds, eating the harsh flint corn unground (it could pierce the intestines), roaming the roads like "animated skeletons," fighting to get into prisons where threre were at least rudimentary meals. Only a few years before, the British had spent £20 million buying up the black slaves from their West Indian masters. Were they now to refuse to pay a mere £4 million (the value of the blighted potatoes) to save the lives of people living on a neighboring island?

In an attempt to ease the famine without actually handing out free food, the government now set up public works. But mobs laboring on the roads ruined the few highways that were in an adequate state (thus making food distribution even more difficult), and their wages, instead of buying food for the starving, fell into the hands of the gombeen-man. Many, too weak, were unable to work at all, and soon this well-meant effort ground to a halt.

Numbers of voluntary workers had been descending on Ireland all along, led by the Quakers. Contributions from private sources were requested, and subscriptions came pouring in, headed by £2,000 from the Queen ($10,000 then and the equivalent of many times that amount in modern terms). Soup kitchens, a familiar sight in impoverished English districts, began to appear in Ireland — a stopgap, which it was hoped would enable tottering men to get back on their feet sufficiently to plant next year's crop. But none of these sufficed to prevent over a million deaths — one out of every eight persons in the population.*

*Compare this with the most severe losses of World War I, those of France: one out of every twenty-nine persons in the population.

WILD GEESE*

Finally, the Irish themselves began to see that it was emigrate or starve. By tens of thousands — ultimately to equal a million and a half, even more than the number of those who died — they streamed out of Ireland to Liverpool and Glasgow, out of those ports and across the Atlantic. Landlords, keen to vacate their land altogether and turn it over to cattle raising (shades of the Enclosure days in England!), offered to pay their tenants' passage to America or Canada. The government also subsidized passage to Canada, in hopes of encouraging settlement there, and as a result fares to Boston or New York were three and a half times as high as those to Montreal. (American ships were also owner-captained, more comfortable, and far safer than their British counterparts.)

Moreover, American cities did not welcome the Irish. Boston, Philadelphia, and New York refused to accept anyone who could be labeled "pauper" and required a bond of $1,000 for every aged or incapable passenger who disembarked. In addition, everyone had to pay $2 "head money" just to come ashore. Then, if an when a man did manage to land and began looking for work, he was likely to be greeted by angry new signs: "No Irish Need Apply."

Nevertheless the Irish poured in. The poorer ones took advantage of the British government's offer, traveled cheaply to Canada, and then slipped across the border to the United States. The Irish had been settling in America since colonial times (New York's St. Patrick's Day parade is older than the country), but never in such numbers. And once the floodgates were opened, the hordes continued to flow steadily across the Atlantic, year after year. The result is that today, next to Anglo-Saxon, German, and Italian, the largest population pool of white Americans is of Irish descent.

The Irish are not natural entrepreneurs. They joined America's mass-labor market and laid railroads, ran streetcars and subways, fought fires. And along with the Chinese laundryman, the German butcher, the Jewish delicatessen owner, and the Italian fruit peddler, the Irish cop became an American institution.

And all this was started by the parasitic fungus *Phytophthora infestans*, which destroyed the potato crop.

---

*A plaintive Irish term for the island's many expatriates.

CONCLUSIONS

Can we learn any lessons, draw any conclusions, from the study of Food in Civilization? We might reflect that there was a great deal in the words written by philosopher Ludwig Feuerbach (1804 – 72): "Do you want to improve people? Then instead of preaching against sin, give them better food. *Der Mensch ist was der isst*. Man is what he eats. Human fare is the foundation of human culture and disposition."

Food certainly has conditioned history. Mankind has only been able to progress from savagery to civilization at the expense of considerable changes in his diet. Sometimes these changes have taken millenia or centuries, sometimes they have been made in a single lifetime. Those archetypal figures of the Industrial Revolution, the Irish navvies * who built the roads of Britain in the 1830's, progressed from the diet of the turf cabin — potatoes and buttermilk — to breakfasts of beefsteaks fried on a red hot shovel. This change had been demanded by the needs placed on them for greater and greater productivity.

As the American writer, Lafcadio Hearn pointed out in the nineteenth century, archaic diet is a great barrier to acquiring modern Western civilization. His words were inspired by the difficulty that his Japanese students found in adapting themselves to the long hours of constant study needed to take their degrees in the subjects taught in the Western-style university of which he was a professor. They are just as applicable to the undeveloped nations of the world today as they were to the Japanese of the Meiji Era. Until everyone enjoys a diet comparable to that acquired by America and Europe, it is idle to talk about progress and civilization.

Hunger can only bring discontent, and discontent revolution, whether the hungry are eighteenth-century French peasants or twentieth-century Polish trade unionists. Long-term failure to achieve an adequate diet can only mean extinction or permanent cultural degradation. In the past, nations have had little control over their dietary destinies. History is full of promising beginnings which ended when the food supplies ran out.

Nowadays, though we have much greater control over our food supplies than ever before, we seem much less emotionally concerned about the sight of hunger than were people in the past. During the eighteenth century the prospect of famine brought mobs out into the streets of English towns to adjust food prices by force or to put an end to the waste of nourishing food in distilleries or the shipment abroad of a

---

*Unskilled laborers, so-called from the men who dug the navigation canals that were Britain's first internal transportation improvement.

harvest surplus. On our television screens today we can see famines as bad or worse than the Great Hunger of Ireland in 1845 – 47, yet these sights seem to produce less of a reaction than they did on eighteenth-century *philosophes* like Count Rumford.

Yet we must react, both emotionally and intellectually, to the problem of hunger, lest we in our turn are condemned by the judgment of history, a judgment that must condemn all but a very few of the great civilizations of the past for preferring the flashy appurtenances of culture to the solid achievement of universal plenty.

14.

Flocks And Herds

It was all very well for scientists such as Ilya Metchnikoff to explain to the public at large that eating meat debilitated the system and that a vegetable diet was far healthier. The public, as a whole, preferred meat. Some may have realized that meat is high in protein; all knew that it was a high-status food. The sizzling beefsteak, the juicy chop, the cut off the joint were, to nineteenth-century folk, every bit as much a token of wealth as a starched collar, a broadcloth coat, or a top hat.

Those nineteenth-century workers who were well paid and in constant employment — rather a small sector who were known as the "labor aristocrats" — immediately invested some of their wealth in food (the best investment anyone can make) and ate beefsteaks. The railway navvies or construction workers even used to eat steak breakfast every day, fried on red-hot shovels over the blacksmith's forge fire. As has already been said, most European workers never tasted meat except in conditions of extraordinary prosperity — such as the seasonal rush in the building trade. They had to make do with fish, a high-protein food, every bit as good, but not what they wanted. Which was a pity, because in the words of a song which Music Hall artiste Marie Lloyd used to sing in the Edwardian era, "A little of what you fancy does you good."

It was a paradox that, while the industrial masses of Europe pined for a mixed grill or for the so-called "Roast Beef of Old England" (how many Englishmen ever ate it?) meat was being thrown away by the ton on the pampas of South America and the pastures of Australia and New Zealand.

What was to bring the meat-starved masses of Europe and their Sunday dinners together was the new era of technology we have already seen, the era that brought the refrigerator ship, the refrigerated car, the freezing plant and the tin can. But the meat economies deserve special comment.

In 1550 Captain Nuflo Chaves brought the first sheep to Argentina; two years later, Juan de Salozer y Espinosa introduced seven cows and one bull, the founding fathers of the mighty herds that were soon to shake the Campo of South America. Spanish colonists settled in the River Plate district of Argentina, and Juan Torre de Vega y Aragon, seeing that the pampas were good cattle country, distributed 4,000 cows and bulls and 4,000 sheep among the colonists.

These flocks and herds multiplied like those of the Hebrew patriarchs. "All the wealth of these inhabitants," writes a seventeenth-century traveler to Argentina, "consists in their animals, which multiply so prodigiously that the plains are covered with them, particularly with bulls, cows, sheep, horses, mares, mules, asses, pigs, deer, and other sorts, in such numbers that, were it not for the dogs that devour the calves and other tender animals, they would devastate the country."

The cattle were the long-horned cows and bulls of Andalusia, the same that were to become famous much farther north as the Texas longhorns. The sheep were of two kinds, the pampa sheep descended from the mountain long-wools imported from Spain, and the criollo, the much degenerated descendants of the Spanish merinos.

So long as Spanish South America remained a continent embargoed from trading with anyone except the home country, there was little hope of improving the breed, but once the Spanish monarchy was overthrown by Napoleon, and the Spaniards rose in revolt, trading with England was established, and the Argentine *estancieros* or ranchers were able to import new stock; they brought in merino sheep and English horned cattle.

To deal with the problems of ranching, the Spanish Americans had evolved the original cowboy, the *gaucho*, from whom the Mexican cowboys of California inherited their skill and equipment. Almost everything the American cowboy wore, or carried on his horse, were

pieces of gear and clothing introduced by the South American *estan-
cieros*. Having said this, I must immediately add that the spirit of the
American cowboy was all his own. He never ceased to be a gentleman.
For an account of the gauchos, I refer to the work of W.H. Hudson, an
English naturalist who spent much of his life in Argentina, where he was
born.

There was one big drawback to ranching, so far as the *estancieros*
were concerned: meat was valueless. A cow was only worth its hide and
tallow. Enormous quantities of hides were exported from all the Spanish
ranching colonies. Richard Dana, in *Two Years Before the Mast*, has
given us an account of his trials and tribulations on the California coast,
loading a cargo of hides.

Meat had so little worth that a *gaucho* would have no qualms about
killing a cow just for a beefsteak. He would, however, skin the cow and
probably try to save the tallow.

Aware of the riches that were going to waste on the pampas, the
Spanish Americans tried to jerk some of the beef, and salt some as well.
In 1794, the livestock breeders of Buenos Aires and Monte Video
presented a petition to the Minister, Don Diego Cardogin, urging that
tallow and jerked beef be exported free, and that the pampas beef trade
be stimulated by the introduction of "eight or nine hundred Irishmen,
bachelors and Roman Catholics." Though the salted meat exports
passing through Buenos Aires customs house had risen to 357,860
quintals by 1862, meat was still such a worthless commodity that flocks
of sheep valued for their pelts were herded to the coast and driven over
the cliffs to kill them before skinning.

Even with live export, salting, jerking, and boiling down to make the
meat extract which German chemist Justus von Liebig (1803 – 73) had
invented, Argentina's herds just kept on growing and growing. An
official census taken in 1875 counted thirteen million cattle and fifty
million sheep. Then, just as the stock breeders despaired of ever dispos-
ing of their surplus, the first attempts at shipping frozen meat began.
After an initial essay by the steamer *Frigorifique* under Captain Tellier,
in 1876, traffic in frozen meat began in earnest in 1883.

This set the *frigorificos*, or freezing plants, on their successful career.
Argentina transformed herself, turning from a purely pastoral country
into a modern industrial nation. In the change, the old ways of the
pampas and the gaucho, which had contained so much that was picturesque and romantic, despite the savagery and cruelty, were to disappear,

and with it much of the pampas, with its once abundant wildlife that had so delighted naturalist Charles Darwin.

This was perhaps a small price for giving the starvelings of Europe what they had always wanted, a slice of beef. The arrival of the *Frigorifique* in Le Havre, France, created one of the biggest sensations in food history. The *Frigorifique* had endured an adventurous voyage, with a collision off the Spanish coast and being forced to put into St. Vincent, Spain, for four months of repairs. Yet so efficient was the ammonia compression machine invented by Carre, and so determined was her captain, Charles Tellier, that her cargo of frozen meat from the Argentine should enter Le Havre in good condition that he actually kept the temperature in the store rooms at 17°F. — something no meat packer had ever done before or since.

The *Frigorifique* docked at Le Havre in 1878 with all her 5,500 carcasses intact. All were sold, and the meat was shared among such diverse social groups as the guests at the Grand Hotel in Paris — who probably just ate the meat for a new sensation — and the conscripts in the garrison troops at Le Havre. The latter had probably never before tasted meat in mess, except possibly horsemeat or donkey. Just as the French once prided themselves on being the best cooks in the world, so there can be little doubt that the worst cooking anywhere occurred in a French army mess.

Nothing succeeds like success, and as soon as the Australian stock breeders and sheep farmers heard about the voyage of the *Frigorifique*, they cabled to London and asked their agents to go to Le Havre to inspect the refrigerator steamer.

Like Argentina, Australia was a country that had been created by the demand for cattle products, such as salt beef, hides, and tallow. But for the cattle industry there would have been no Australia as we know it today. And this is all the more remarkable, as the country had begun life as a corral or pen for quite a different kind of livestock — human beings.

Australia had been carefully charted by that indefatigable explorer, Captain James Cook, in 1769 – 70. Its survey came at a time when Britain was about to part company with the American colonies, which had hitherto served, among other purposes, as a dumping ground for convicts. In those days there were no prisons for harboring criminals sentenced to long terms. Such sentences were not imposed, except for treason. Prisoners lay in jail awaiting trial, and sentence — usually to the gallows. Transportation abroad, or sending convicts overseas as "indentured" prisoners or white slaves, was supposedly a more humane penalty than hanging.

After recognition of American independence by the Peace of Paris, the British government expressed the hope that, as before, British convicts might continue to be sent to the American mainland. Benjamin Franklin is supposed to have given the following reply. "Send us convicts, and we will give you rattlesnakes in exchange." The British cabinet was nonplused. Where else could the convicts be sent? Obviously, they could not remain in Britain, where there were no prisons to contain them.

Then somebody had a brain wave. What about the new continent in the South Pacific which Cook had surveyed. Might it not be possible to send convicts there? Australia had one enormous advantage as a convict settlement. It was about as far from home as anyone could go without turning back on the journey around the globe. No convict sent to Australia was ever likely to escape from it, much less make his way back to England.

In May, 1781, a fleet left England on what was surely the strangest venture of colonization known to history. It was bound for Port Jackson, at Botany Bay, New South Wales, which had been one of Captain Cook's anchorages. About half the complement of the ships — old army transports — were convicts, the other half soldiers sent to guard them.

From the punitive point of view the expedition was an immense success. Life for the convicts was twice as hard as it would have been in America. There, labor had been in such short supply that few questions were asked about a man's past, once he had served his indentures. The ex-convicts had thrived in the American colonies; some female convicts had even founded "first families."

From the financial point of view, however, the settlement of Botany Bay was a disaster. It cost the English taxpayer £1,000 per convict to ship them to the Southern Hemisphere. This vast sum — at least $14,000 in U.S. values — made the government feel that unless some other plan could be devised to make settlement of the new continent pay, transportation would have to be abandoned.

England's solution to her $14,000 tourists was to send out *free* settlers who could begin to produce goods that could be shipped to Britain under the old colonial system and that would pay the expense of convict transportation. There were only four products which Australia could provide: beef, mutton, hides and sheepskins. The interior of the continent was partly desert, partly luxuriant grassland and blue-gum forests. Wherever water could be found, free settlers, usually helped by convicts and under the direction of squatters or ranchers who had settled outside the narrow state boundaries, built stations and commenced to graze great herds of sheep and cattle.

Conditions in the great Australian outback or range were strangely like, yet also very unlike, those of an American cattle area such as Texas. The biggest difference has already been noticed. Whereas all the inhabitants of old Texas were free (except for African slaves) many of the shepherds, stockmen, and men employed on the Australian farms were "government men" or assigned convicts. Some settlers treated their convicts well, gave them ample rations and indulged them in other ways, such as by handing out the only Australian luxuries, tobacco and tea.

Others treated them harshly, sending them to the nearest district police court and having them sentenced to fifty, seventy, or a hundred lashes. Sometimes the settlers were so cruel that their captives escaped into the bush, and became the dreaded "bushrangers" — outlaws who attacked stations and held up stage coaches (which, by the way, had to be imported from America, as no English stage could stand the pounding across the rough Australian terrain).

The bushrangers were a much greater menace than the aborigines, people of a very primitive stage of development who were never a bar to effective settlement. By the 1840's parties of settlers could be seen riding alongside their drays, or wagons, and driving great herds of sheep or cattle into the interior, looking for good pasture land and water.

When they stopped for the night, as they did every fourteen miles or so, they would hobble the oxen and build a stockade of gum trees, into which they would drive the sheep. The sheep had to be protected in this way, for fear of the dingoes, or wild dogs. These dingoes, domesticated dogs which had gone wild, would otherwise scatter the sheep. The stockmen and shepherds would then build a hut of gum logs, strip off the bark, and proceed to cook their evening meal on a fire made with the fallen wood.

The menu was always the same, "damper," salt beef, fresh mutton and tea — except, as one Australian bushman or wanderer remarked, when they "had tea, fresh mutton, salt beef and damper for a change." Damper was bread made without yeast, just a flour-and-salt mixture, baked in thin cakes laid on top of hot charcoal beaten down flat for the purpose. The stockmen or Australian cowboys, and the shepherds, drank a lot of tea, which they boiled in billy cans on the fire. It was the only drink that would effectively quench a thirst in the hot Australian summer.

The settlers would drive their sheep and cattle farther and farther into the interior, stopping only to ferry them over rivers in boats, till they reached a spot which the squatter chose as a permanent station, a place where there was always plenty of grass and water.

There the party would build "gunyahs" or huts until they could construct more permanent station house of gum logs. The cattle and sheep run was rented from the government. A tract of two hundred or more square miles could be hired for £10 a year, along with a tax of threepence a head on the cattle.

A herd of two thousand or so would be under the charge of a stockman, whose business it was to get them accustomed to their new run from the old pastures whence they had been driven. Once the cattle got used to the range, they would not leave it. The stockman's duties then became a lot easier, because all he had to do was ride around visiting the mobs of a hundred cattle, each of which had its own grazing ground near water. He had to round up any strays, which other settlers were always eager to rustle (especially if they had not been branded). The stockman wore trousers and shirt, and over the shirt a blue flannel shirt or blouse. He wore a hat woven from cabbage-tree leaves when the sun shone, as it usually did, and a soft felt hat when it rained.

He carried an enormous whip with a lash ten feet or more in length, and on approaching a station, he cracked the whiplash to signal his arrival. This was the moment for the people at the station to "sling the pot," or start cooking his meal. Australia was the most hospitable country in the world, partly because there were no pubs for hundreds of miles apart. Even an innkeeper would give his guests free meals if they had no money, however, because he knew that someday he might be wandering in the bush and be glad to have a meal given to him by strangers. The stockman never carried pistols, which were too expensive for the average Australian, though bushrangers were armed. He would, however, carry a small carbine, to defend himself against his most dangerous enemies, the black snake, often met with in the bush, and which would rise on its coils to the height of a man's face and strike at him.

Another difference between the Australian outback and the American

West was that there was no animosity between sheep owners and cattle men. The two were often the same person, a wealthy squatter who employed stockmen, who went their leisurely rounds, and shepherds who were out every day with their flocks, to guard against dingoes. At night the sheep would begin to move toward their pens of their own accord, and if they did not do so quickly enough, the shepherd's dog, a silky-haired, spaniel-like creature, would hurry them up.

Shepherding was such unskilled work, not even requiring the ability to ride a horse, that many who became shepherds were "remittance" men, young men of good family in England who had got into some kind of scrape, and were sent off to the colonies as a way of getting rid of them. They were paid a regular allowance or "remittance" by post, so long as they remained in Australia.

Remittance men could hope that their relatives would relent and ask them to return to England; many of those who were assigned had been transported to Australia for the rest of their lives.

The development of the Australian sheep industry came at a very opportune time. In 1852, the textile industry in England was expanding rapidly, and the mills could absorb the forty-five million pounds of wool that Australia was producing annually. At about the same time, a California miner named Hargreaves discovered gold in Australia. Immigrants poured into the country at the rate of two thousand a week, eager to make new discoveries themselves. Their arrival enabled the settlers to sell the beef and mutton that had previously gone to waste. The introduction of the refrigerated food ship, and the canning factory, completed the development of the Australian economy.

Thereafter Australia became the larder of Europe. The growth of its monoculture of meat raising elevated it to a point where it had enough capital to develop gold mining and other industries, and also absorb the influx of population that followed the great gold rush. Thereafter it began to diversify, ceasing to be a mono-food culture. But for the introduction of the merino sheep into Australia when George Washington and George III were interesting themselves in them, but for the arrival of longhorn cattle from the Cape, but for the government decision to allow free settlement of the interior, Australia might have become, not a Western, but an Eastern country.

The Chinese had almost certainly discovered it first, and but for the Japanese decision to withdraw protection for the Japanese colonies forming in the Pacific in the seventeenth century, the vast continent might have become an Asiatic domain.

It was the European desire for more beef and mutton, first smoked, then tinned and frozen, which had drawn Australia back into the Western orbit. It was stock raising and shepherding that had created the Australian spirit, a frontier ethic not unlike that of the American West. It was the task of supplying a continent with cattle and sheep that had made the Australians what they are today. Just one indication of the effect of beef and mutton on Australian history is the national song (as opposed to the national anthem). "Waltzing Matilda" is a song about a swagman, or bushman, tramping through the bush in search of work. The swagman was probably a remittance man, because he sings a song about happier days when he went waltzing with Matilda, steals a sheep so as to have something to eat, only to be surprised by a squatter "riding his thoroughbred" and a posse of the dreaded Australian Mounted Police — the equivalent of the Texas Rangers or Canadian Mounted Police. Rather than face the certain flogging of a hundred lashes or more, the swagman throws himself into a billabong, or lake, and drowns himself.

It is a sad song, which realistically reflects a bitter era in which food production by convict labor, at the behest of an imported English aristocracy, had turned a country that is a paradise on earth into something very much the opposite, and just because it is a sad song, it seems a good note on which to close the troubled history of food.